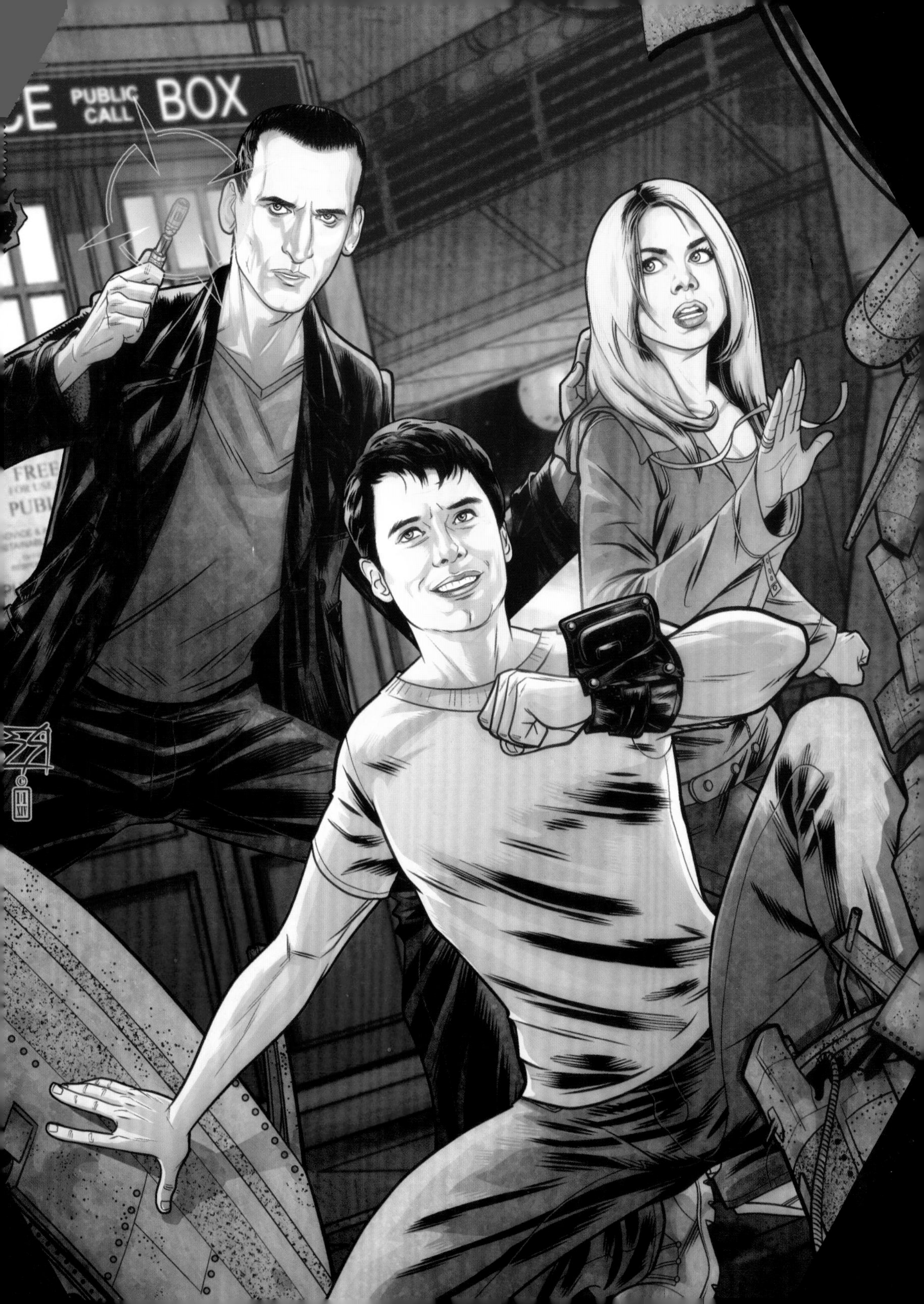

PUBLIC CALL
BOX
FREE

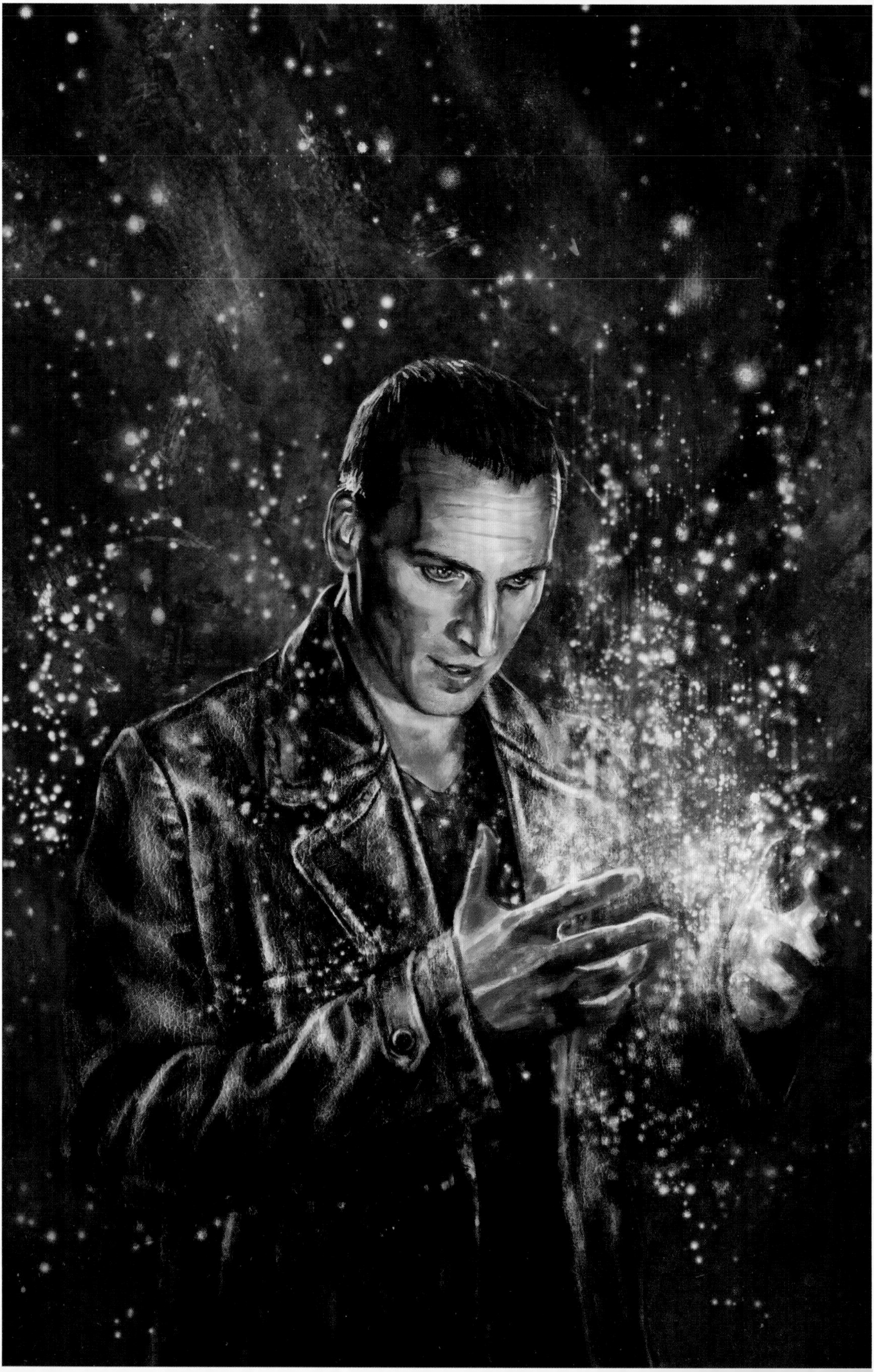

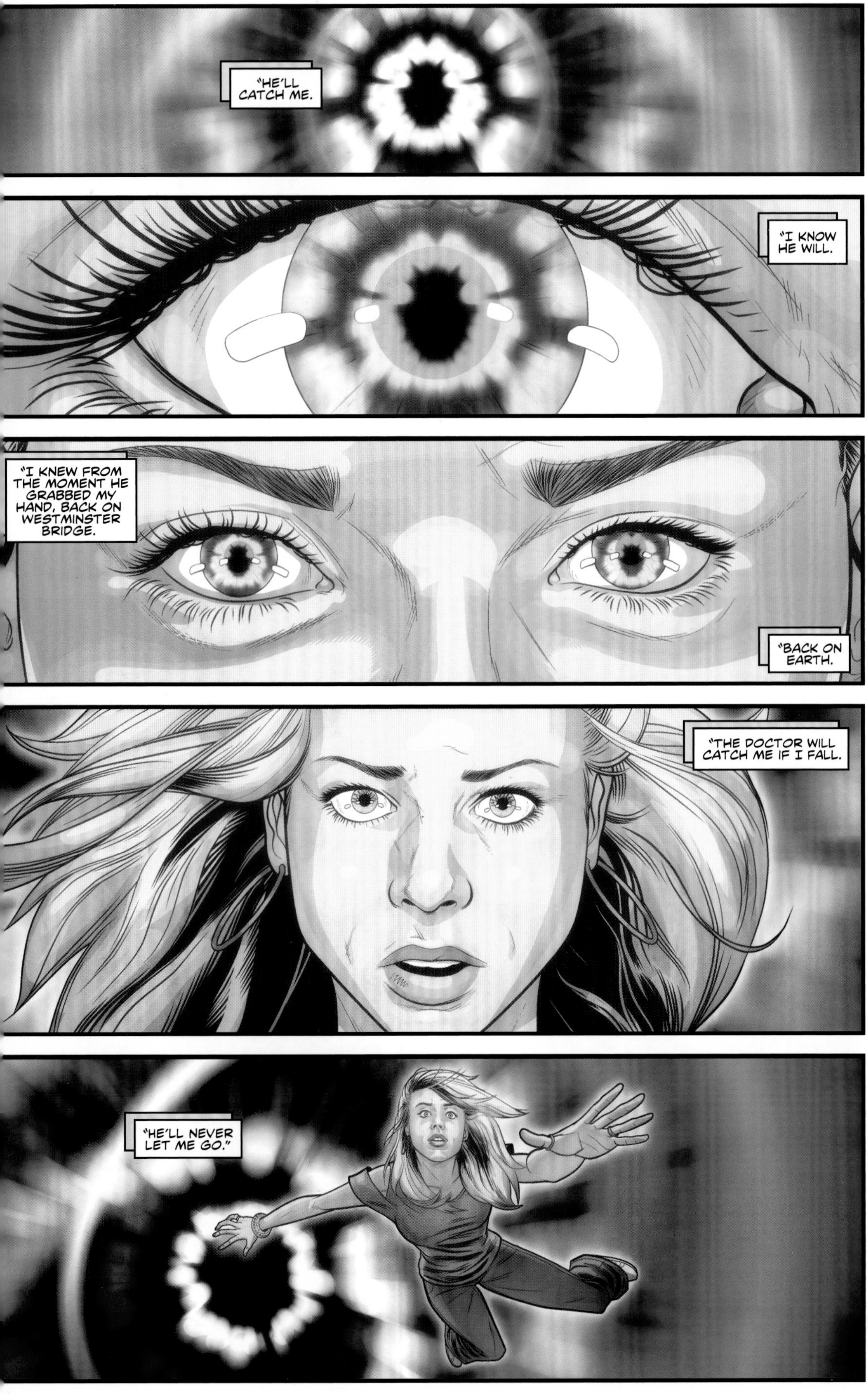
"HE'LL CATCH ME.
"I KNOW HE WILL.
"I KNEW FROM THE MOMENT HE GRABBED MY HAND, BACK ON WESTMINSTER BRIDGE.
"BACK ON EARTH.
"THE DOCTOR WILL CATCH ME IF I FALL.
"HE'LL NEVER LET ME GO."

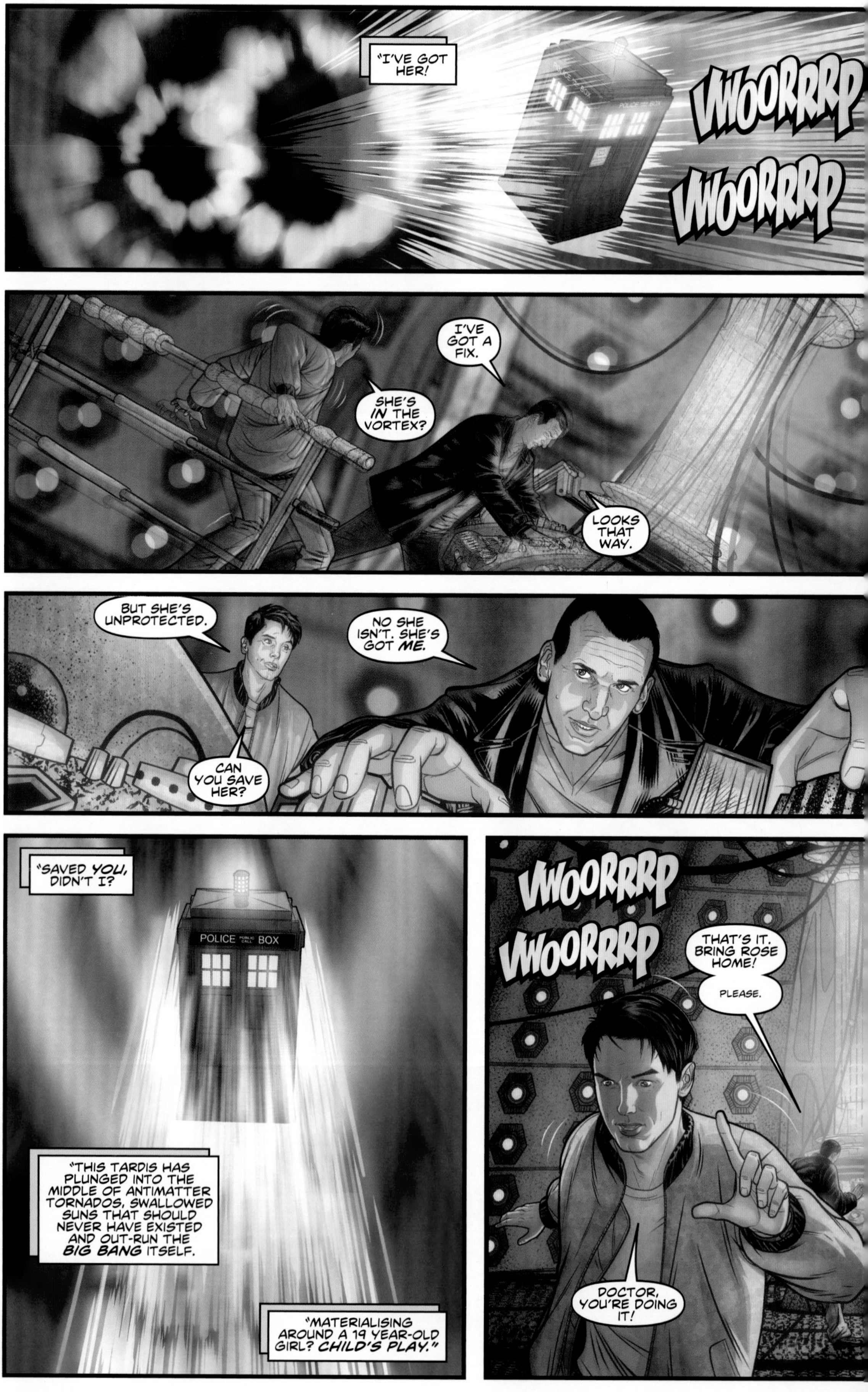
"I'VE GOT HER!
VWOORRRP
VWOORRRP
I'VE GOT A FIX.
SHE'S IN THE VORTEX?
LOOKS THAT WAY.
BUT SHE'S UNPROTECTED.
NO SHE ISN'T. SHE'S GOT ME.
CAN YOU SAVE HER?
"SAVED YOU, DIDN'T I?
POLICE BOX
"THIS TARDIS HAS PLUNGED INTO THE MIDDLE OF ANTIMATTER TORNADOS, SWALLOWED SUNS THAT SHOULD NEVER HAVE EXISTED AND OUT-RUN THE BIG BANG ITSELF.
"MATERIALISING AROUND A 19 YEAR-OLD GIRL? CHILD'S PLAY."
VWOORRRP
VWOORRRP
THAT'S IT. BRING ROSE HOME!
PLEASE.
DOCTOR, YOU'RE DOING IT!

VVOORRRP
VVOORRRP

VVOORRRP
VVOORRRP

VVOORRRP

NO!

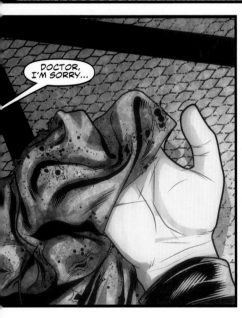

DOCTOR, I'M SORRY...

IT... IT MUST HAVE BEEN THE *TIME WINDS.*

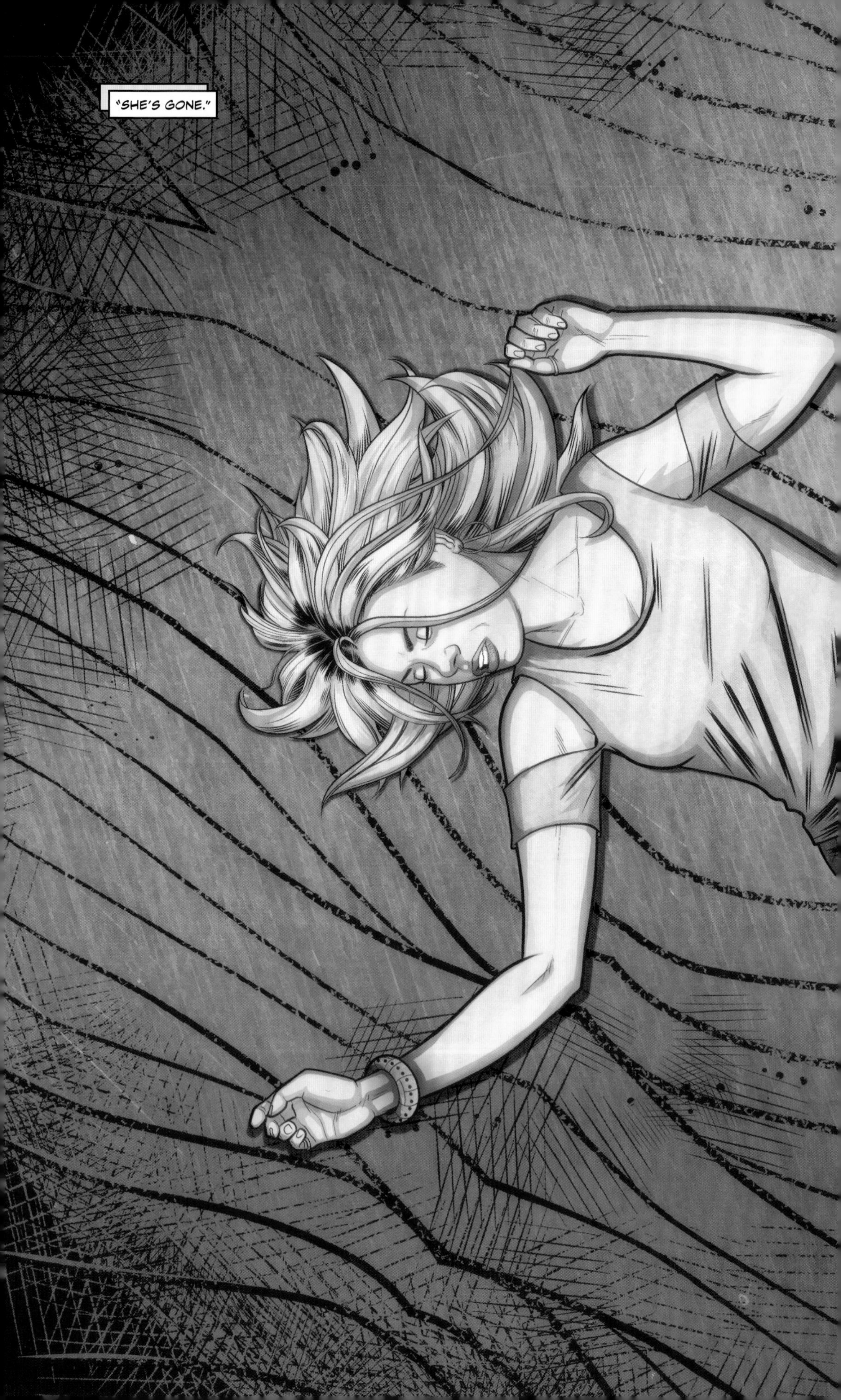
"SHE'S GONE."

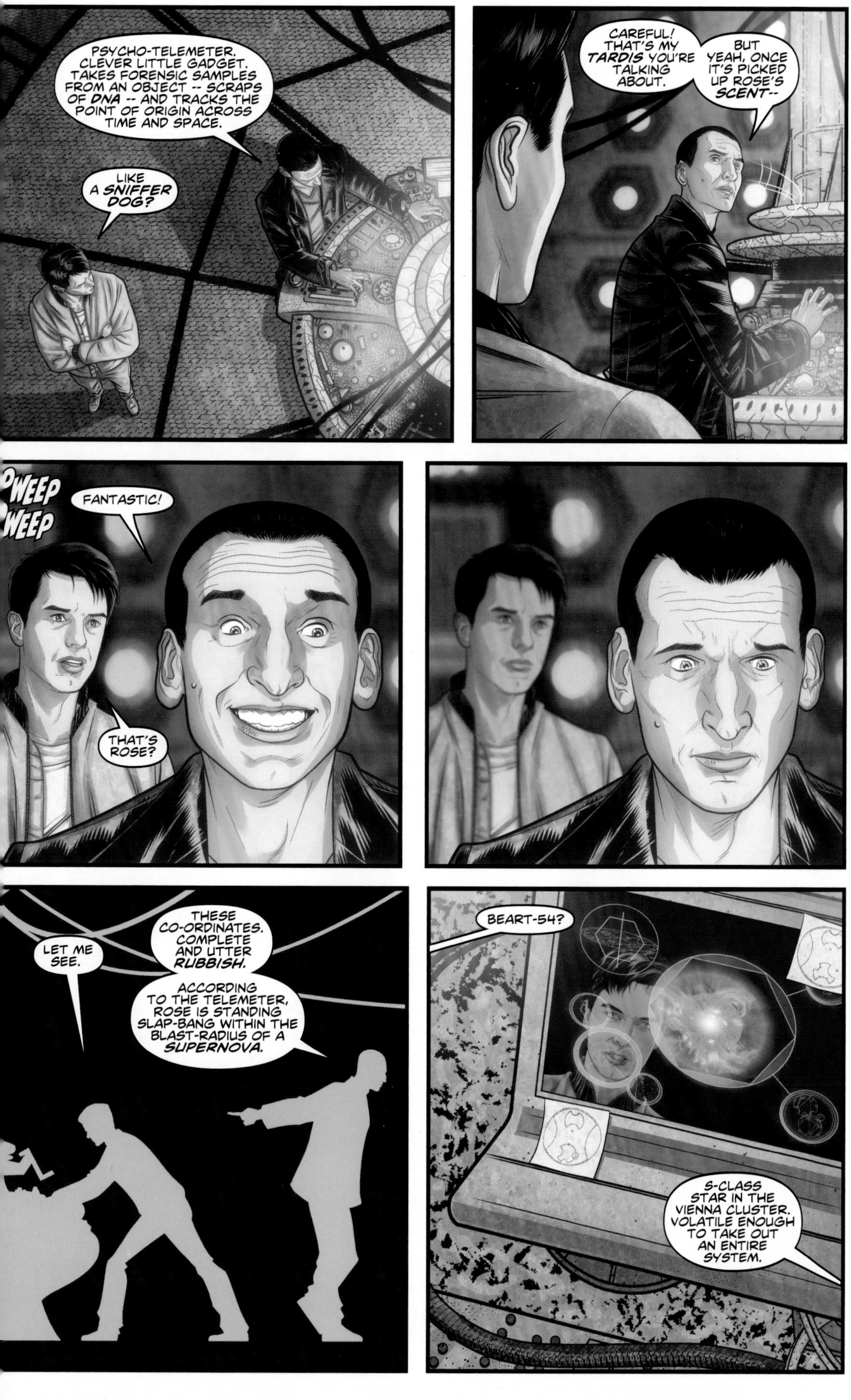
PSYCHO-TELEMETER. CLEVER LITTLE GADGET. TAKES FORENSIC SAMPLES FROM AN OBJECT -- SCRAPS OF DNA -- AND TRACKS THE POINT OF ORIGIN ACROSS TIME AND SPACE.
LIKE A SNIFFER DOG?
CAREFUL! THAT'S MY TARDIS YOU'RE TALKING ABOUT.
BUT YEAH, ONCE IT'S PICKED UP ROSE'S SCENT--
WEEP WEEP
FANTASTIC!
THAT'S ROSE?
LET ME SEE.
THESE CO-ORDINATES. COMPLETE AND UTTER RUBBISH.
ACCORDING TO THE TELEMETER, ROSE IS STANDING SLAP-BANG WITHIN THE BLAST-RADIUS OF A SUPERNOVA.
BEART-54?
S-CLASS STAR IN THE VIENNA CLUSTER. VOLATILE ENOUGH TO TAKE OUT AN ENTIRE SYSTEM.

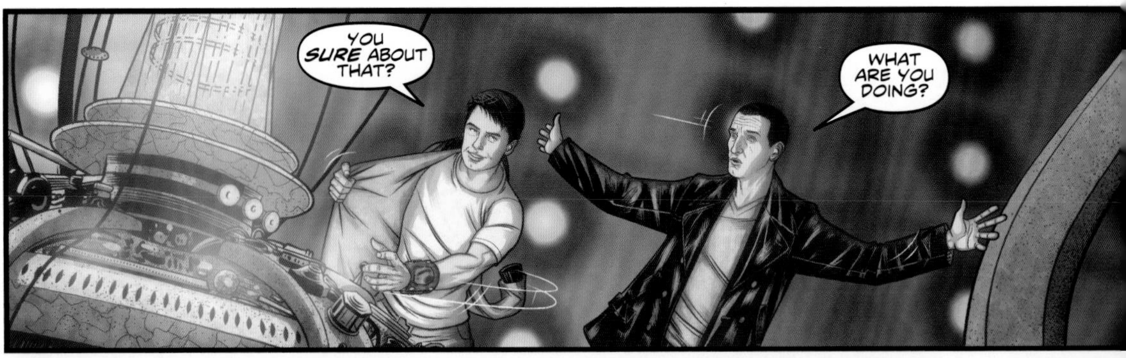
YOU SURE ABOUT THAT?
WHAT ARE YOU DOING?

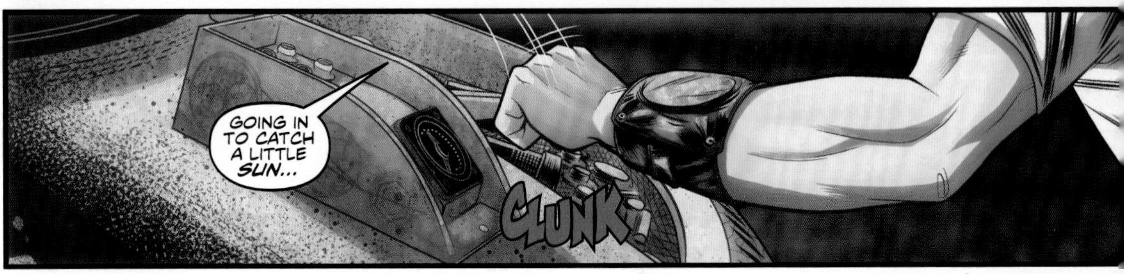
GOING IN TO CATCH A LITTLE SUN...
CLUNK!

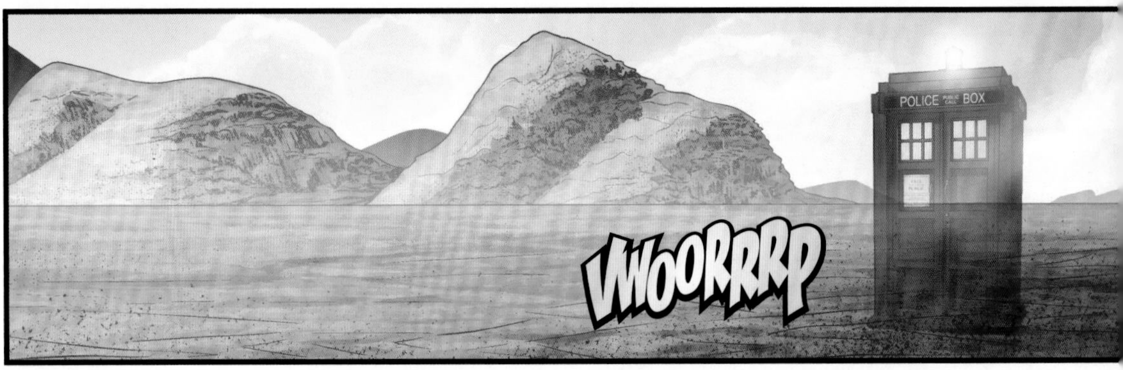
POLICE PUBLIC CALL BOX
VWOORRRP

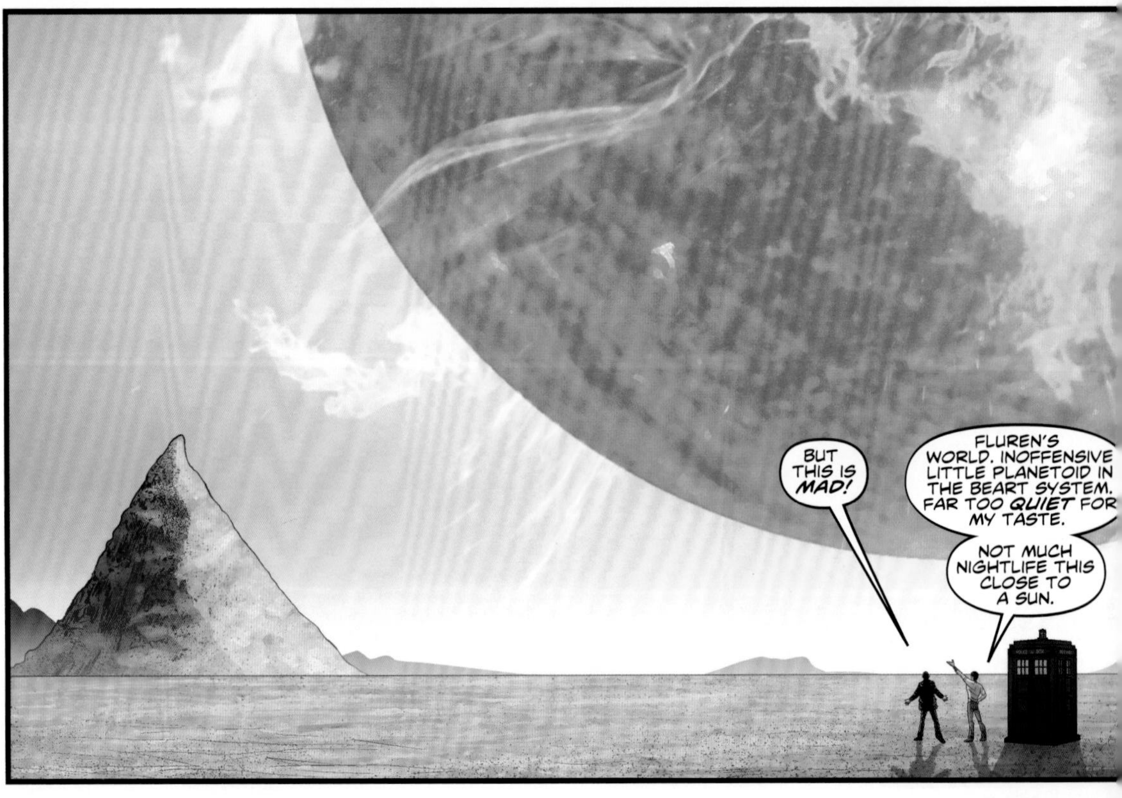
FLUREN'S WORLD. INOFFENSIVE LITTLE PLANETOID IN THE BEART SYSTEM. FAR TOO QUIET FOR MY TASTE.
BUT THIS IS MAD!
NOT MUCH NIGHTLIFE THIS CLOSE TO A SUN.

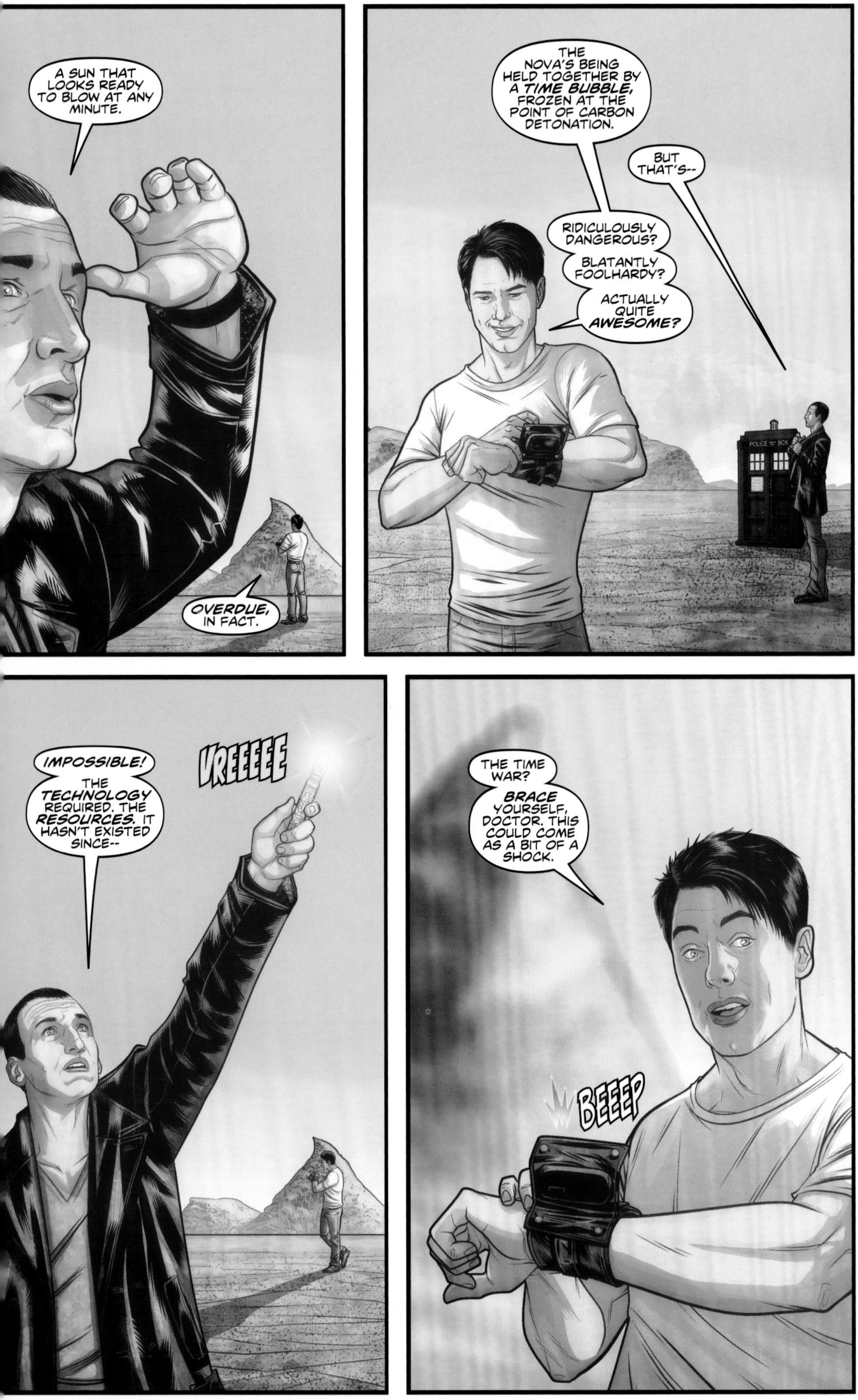
A SUN THAT LOOKS READY TO BLOW AT ANY MINUTE.
OVERDUE, IN FACT.
THE NOVA'S BEING HELD TOGETHER BY A TIME BUBBLE, FROZEN AT THE POINT OF CARBON DETONATION.
BUT THAT'S--
RIDICULOUSLY DANGEROUS?
BLATANTLY FOOLHARDY?
ACTUALLY QUITE AWESOME?
POLICE BOX
IMPOSSIBLE!
THE TECHNOLOGY REQUIRED. THE RESOURCES. IT HASN'T EXISTED SINCE--
VREEEEE
THE TIME WAR?
BRACE YOURSELF, DOCTOR. THIS COULD COME AS A BIT OF A SHOCK.
BEEEP

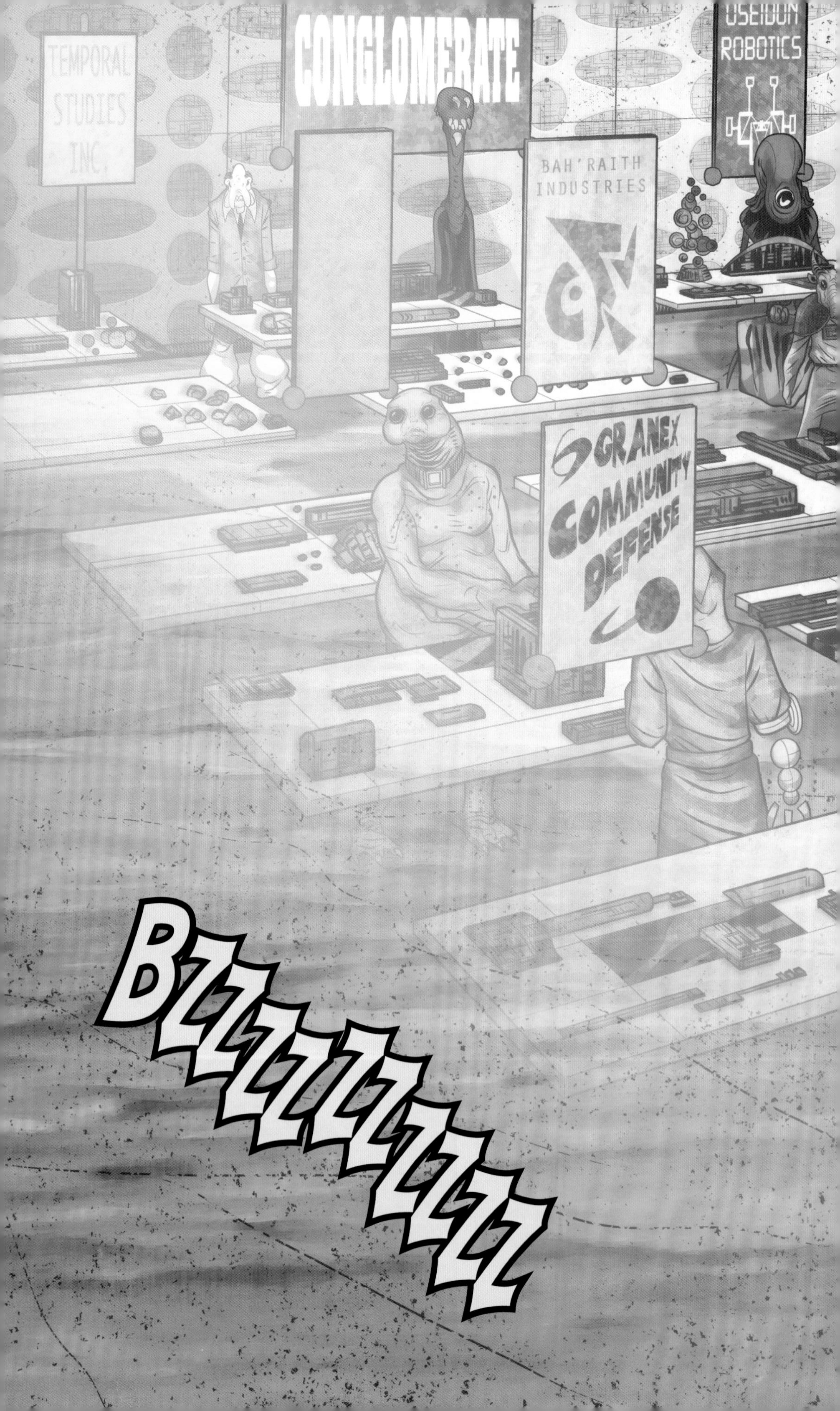
TEMPORAL STUDIES INC.
CONGLOMERATE
USEIDON ROBOTICS
BAH'RAITH INDUSTRIES
GRANEX COMMUNITY DEFENSE
BZZZZZZZZZZ

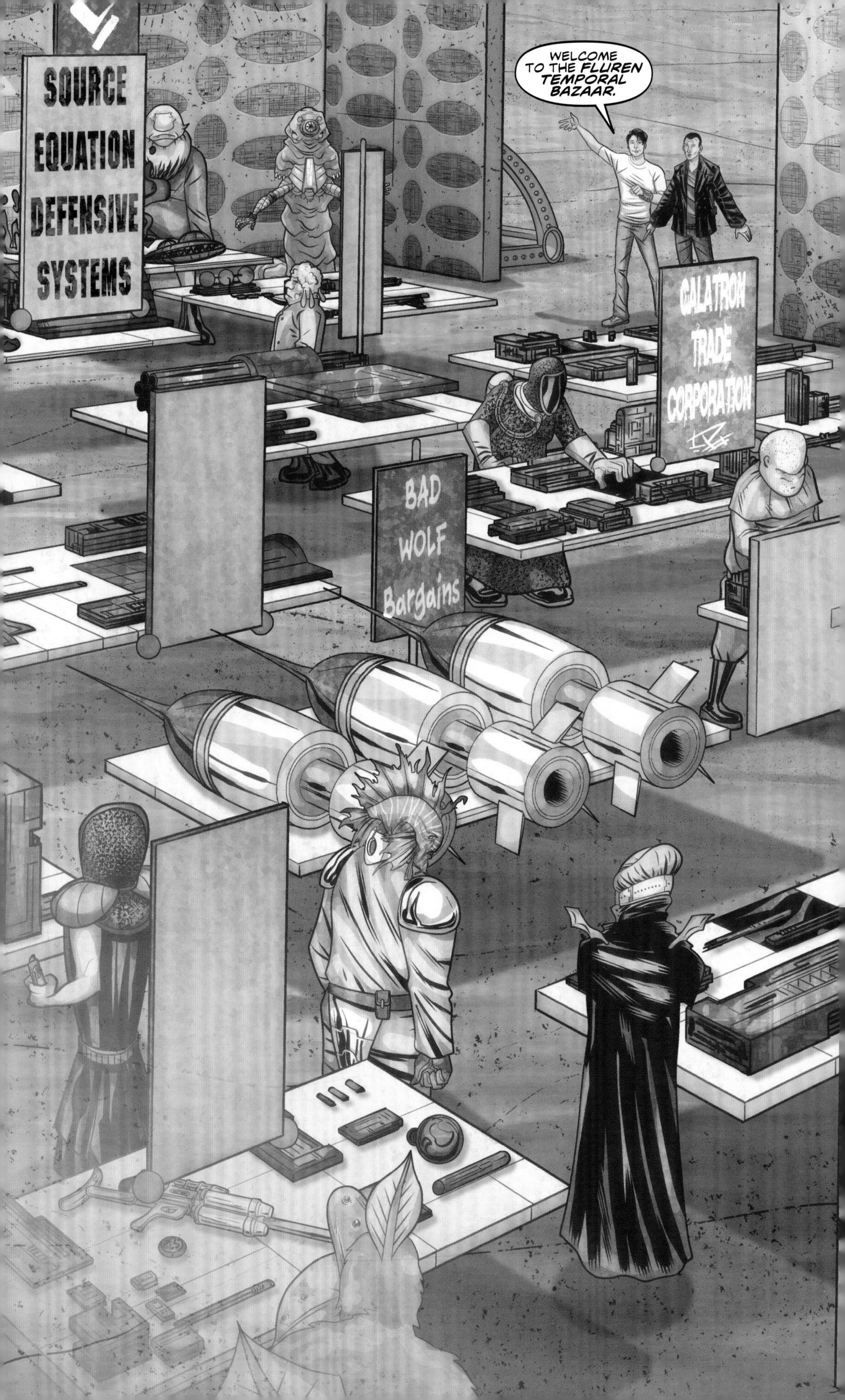
SOURCE EQUATION DEFENSIVE SYSTEMS
WELCOME TO THE FLUREN TEMPORAL BAZAAR.
GALATRON TRADE CORPORATION
BAD WOLF Bargains

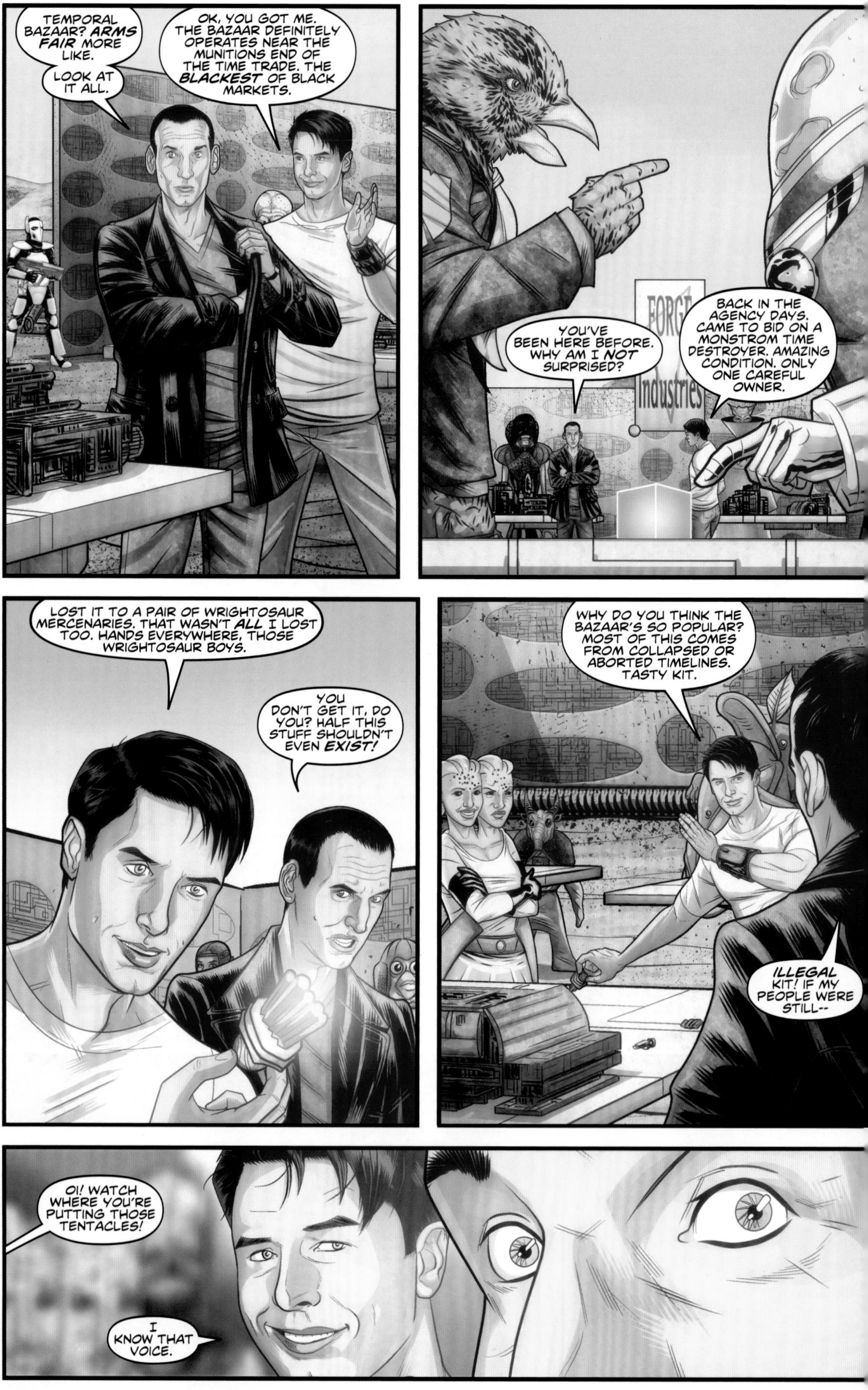

TEMPORAL BAZAAR? ARMS FAIR MORE LIKE.
LOOK AT IT ALL.
OK, YOU GOT ME. THE BAZAAR DEFINITELY OPERATES NEAR THE MUNITIONS END OF THE TIME TRADE. THE BLACKEST OF BLACK MARKETS.
FORGE Industries
YOU'VE BEEN HERE BEFORE. WHY AM I NOT SURPRISED?
BACK IN THE AGENCY DAYS. CAME TO BID ON A MONSTROM TIME DESTROYER. AMAZING CONDITION. ONLY ONE CAREFUL OWNER.
LOST IT TO A PAIR OF WRIGHTOSAUR MERCENARIES. THAT WASN'T ALL I LOST TOO. HANDS EVERYWHERE, THOSE WRIGHTOSAUR BOYS.
YOU DON'T GET IT, DO YOU? HALF THIS STUFF SHOULDN'T EVEN EXIST!
WHY DO YOU THINK THE BAZAAR'S SO POPULAR? MOST OF THIS COMES FROM COLLAPSED OR ABORTED TIMELINES. TASTY KIT.
ILLEGAL KIT! IF MY PEOPLE WERE STILL--
OI! WATCH WHERE YOU'RE PUTTING THOSE TENTACLES!
I KNOW THAT VOICE.

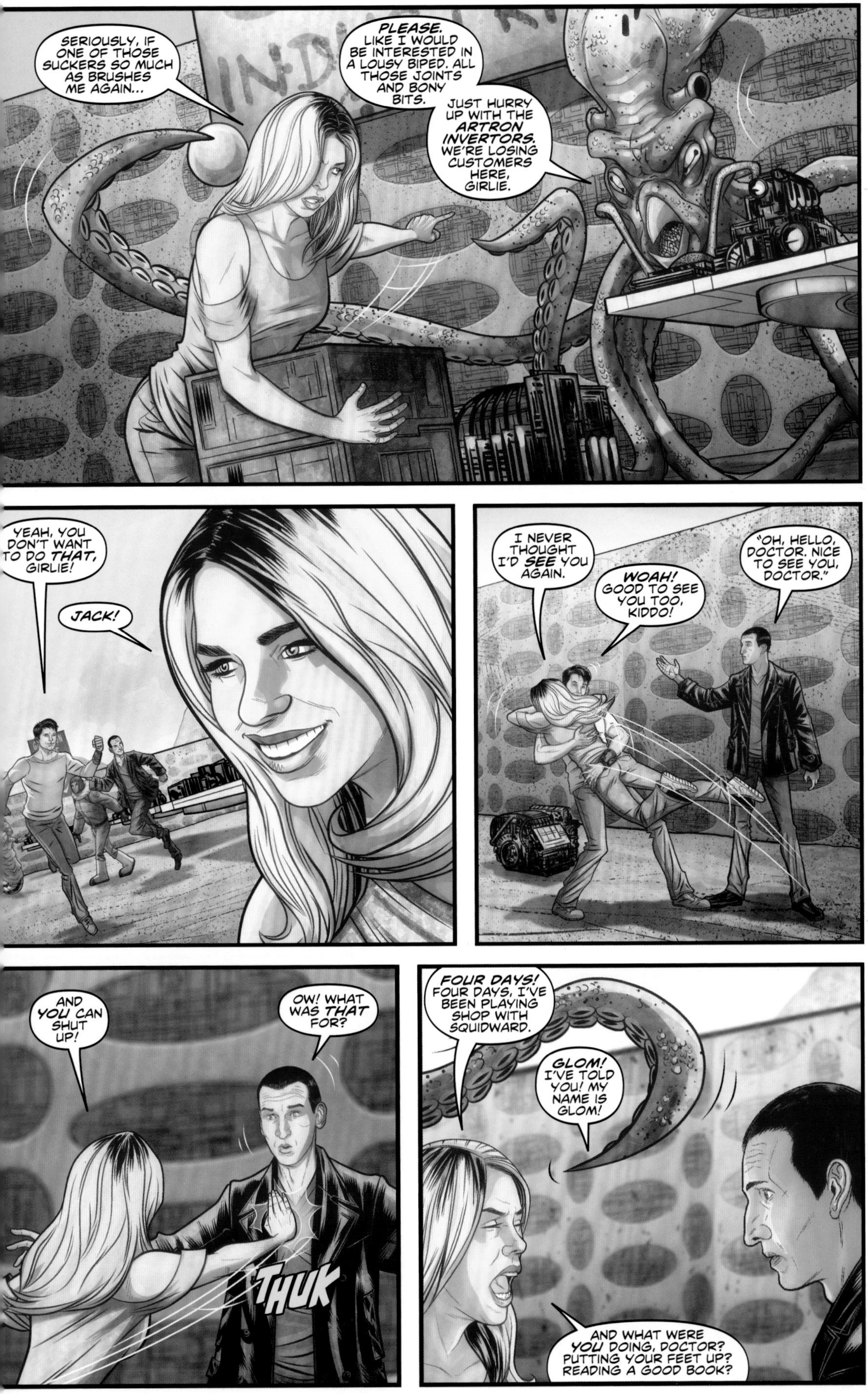
SERIOUSLY, IF ONE OF THOSE SUCKERS SO MUCH AS BRUSHES ME AGAIN...
PLEASE. LIKE I WOULD BE INTERESTED IN A LOUSY BIPED. ALL THOSE JOINTS AND BONY BITS.
JUST HURRY UP WITH THE *ARTRON INVERTORS.* WE'RE LOSING CUSTOMERS HERE, GIRLIE.
YEAH, YOU DON'T WANT TO DO *THAT*, GIRLIE!
JACK!
I NEVER THOUGHT I'D *SEE* YOU AGAIN.
WOAH! GOOD TO SEE YOU TOO, KIDDO!
"OH, HELLO, DOCTOR. NICE TO SEE YOU, DOCTOR."
AND *YOU* CAN SHUT UP!
OW! WHAT WAS *THAT* FOR?
THUK
FOUR DAYS! FOUR DAYS, I'VE BEEN PLAYING SHOP WITH SQUIDWARD.
GLOM! I'VE TOLD YOU! MY NAME IS GLOM!
AND WHAT WERE *YOU* DOING, DOCTOR? PUTTING YOUR FEET UP? READING A GOOD BOOK?

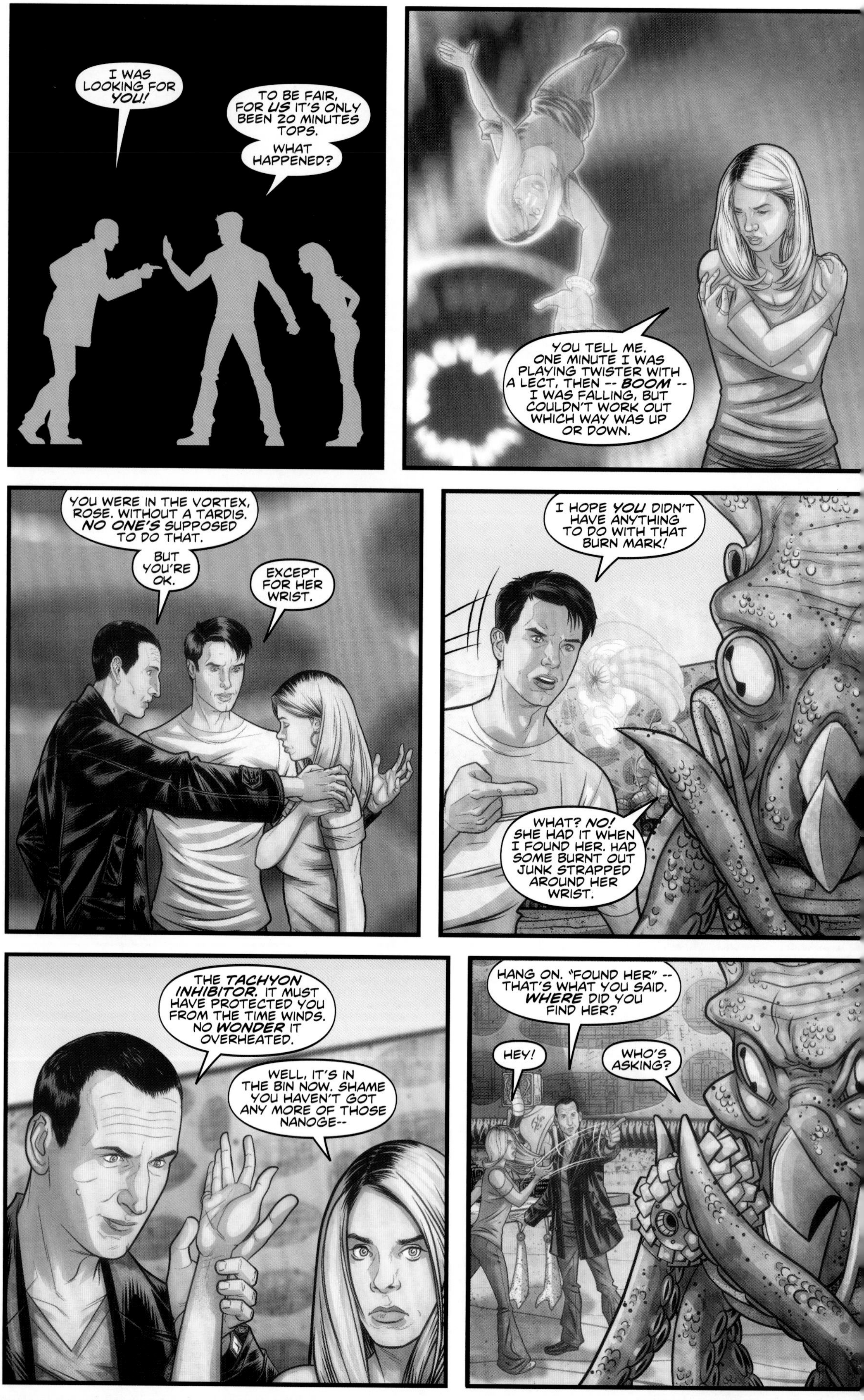
I WAS LOOKING FOR YOU!
TO BE FAIR, FOR US IT'S ONLY BEEN 20 MINUTES TOPS.
WHAT HAPPENED?
YOU TELL ME. ONE MINUTE I WAS PLAYING TWISTER WITH A LECT, THEN -- BOOM -- I WAS FALLING, BUT COULDN'T WORK OUT WHICH WAY WAS UP OR DOWN.
YOU WERE IN THE VORTEX, ROSE. WITHOUT A TARDIS. NO ONE'S SUPPOSED TO DO THAT.
BUT YOU'RE OK.
EXCEPT FOR HER WRIST.
I HOPE YOU DIDN'T HAVE ANYTHING TO DO WITH THAT BURN MARK!
WHAT? NO! SHE HAD IT WHEN I FOUND HER. HAD SOME BURNT OUT JUNK STRAPPED AROUND HER WRIST.
THE TACHYON INHIBITOR. IT MUST HAVE PROTECTED YOU FROM THE TIME WINDS. NO WONDER IT OVERHEATED.
WELL, IT'S IN THE BIN NOW. SHAME YOU HAVEN'T GOT ANY MORE OF THOSE NANOGE--
HANG ON. "FOUND HER" -- THAT'S WHAT YOU SAID. WHERE DID YOU FIND HER?
HEY!
WHO'S ASKING?

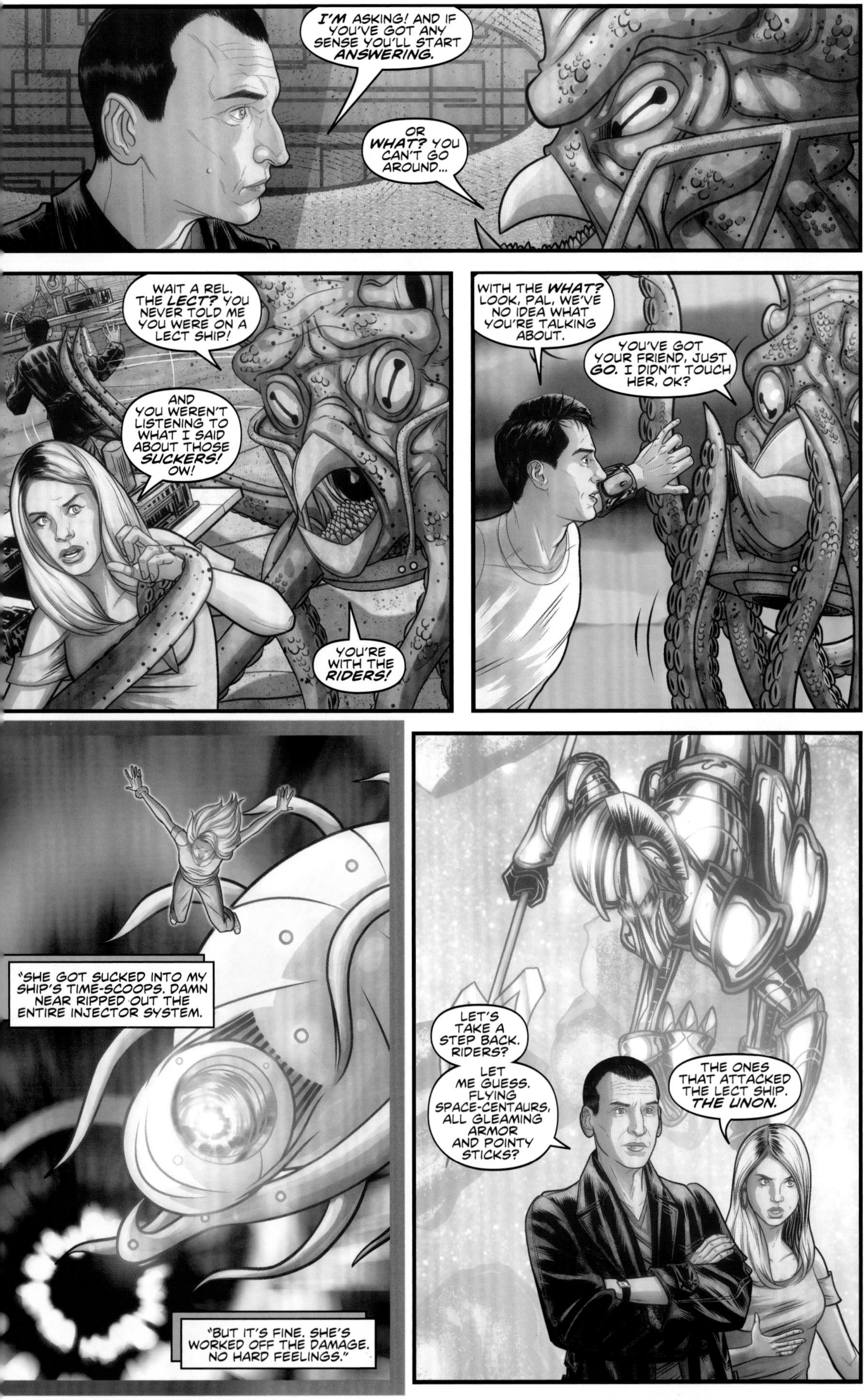

I'M ASKING! AND IF YOU'VE GOT ANY SENSE YOU'LL START ANSWERING.
OR WHAT? YOU CAN'T GO AROUND...
WAIT A REL. THE LECT? YOU NEVER TOLD ME YOU WERE ON A LECT SHIP!
AND YOU WEREN'T LISTENING TO WHAT I SAID ABOUT THOSE SUCKERS! OW!
YOU'RE WITH THE RIDERS!
WITH THE WHAT? LOOK, PAL, WE'VE NO IDEA WHAT YOU'RE TALKING ABOUT.
YOU'VE GOT YOUR FRIEND, JUST GO. I DIDN'T TOUCH HER, OK?
"SHE GOT SUCKED INTO MY SHIP'S TIME-SCOOPS. DAMN NEAR RIPPED OUT THE ENTIRE INJECTOR SYSTEM.
"BUT IT'S FINE. SHE'S WORKED OFF THE DAMAGE. NO HARD FEELINGS."
LET'S TAKE A STEP BACK. RIDERS?
LET ME GUESS. FLYING SPACE-CENTAURS, ALL GLEAMING ARMOR AND POINTY STICKS?
THE ONES THAT ATTACKED THE LECT SHIP. THE UNON.

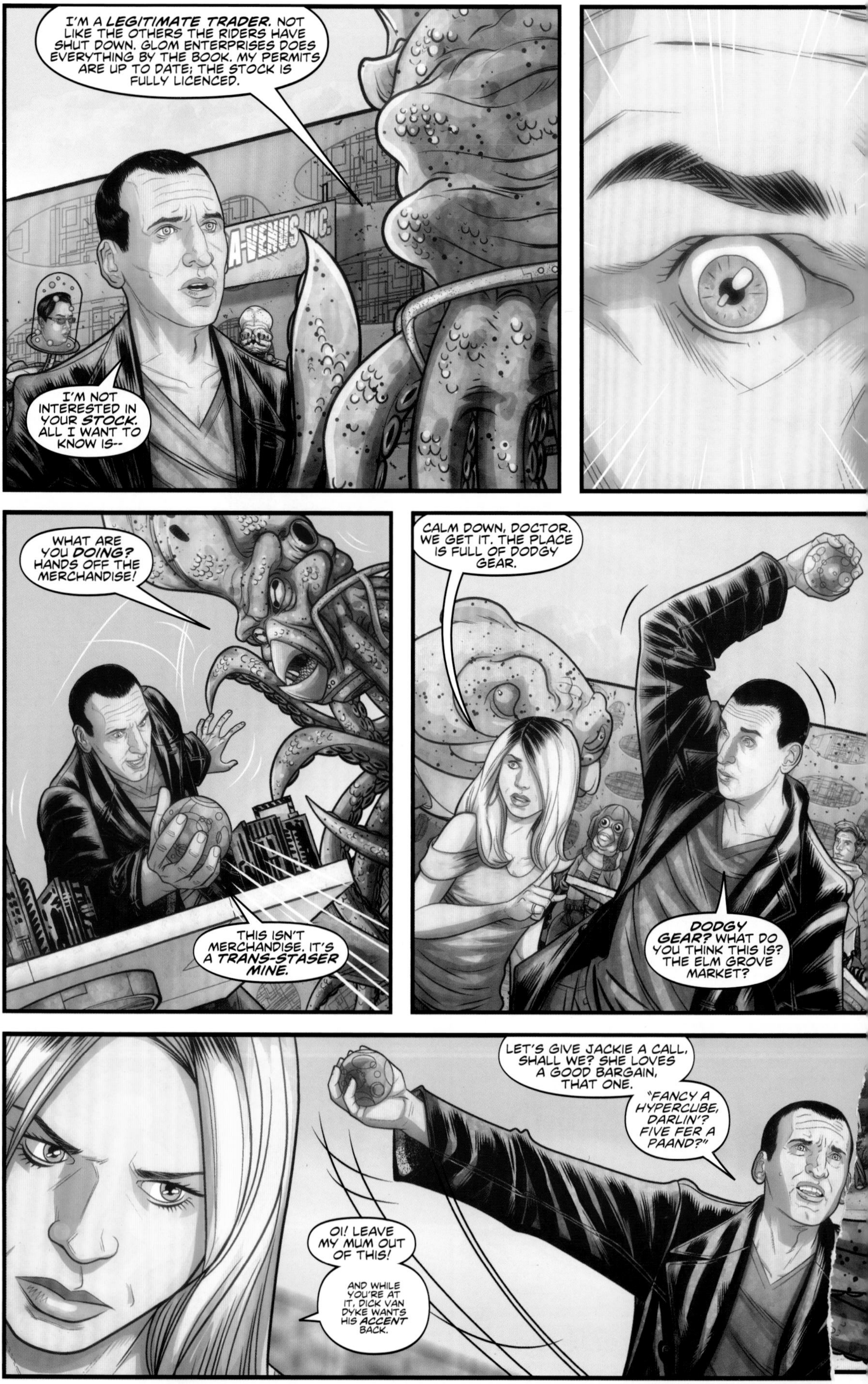

I'M A LEGITIMATE TRADER. NOT LIKE THE OTHERS THE RIDERS HAVE SHUT DOWN. GLOM ENTERPRISES DOES EVERYTHING BY THE BOOK. MY PERMITS ARE UP TO DATE; THE STOCK IS FULLY LICENCED.
A-VENUS INC.
I'M NOT INTERESTED IN YOUR STOCK. ALL I WANT TO KNOW IS--
WHAT ARE YOU DOING? HANDS OFF THE MERCHANDISE!
THIS ISN'T MERCHANDISE. IT'S A TRANS-STASER MINE.
CALM DOWN, DOCTOR. WE GET IT. THE PLACE IS FULL OF DODGY GEAR.
DODGY GEAR? WHAT DO YOU THINK THIS IS? THE ELM GROVE MARKET?
LET'S GIVE JACKIE A CALL, SHALL WE? SHE LOVES A GOOD BARGAIN, THAT ONE.
"FANCY A HYPERCUBE, DARLIN'? FIVE FER A PAAND?"
OI! LEAVE MY MUM OUT OF THIS!
AND WHILE YOU'RE AT IT, DICK VAN DYKE WANTS HIS ACCENT BACK.

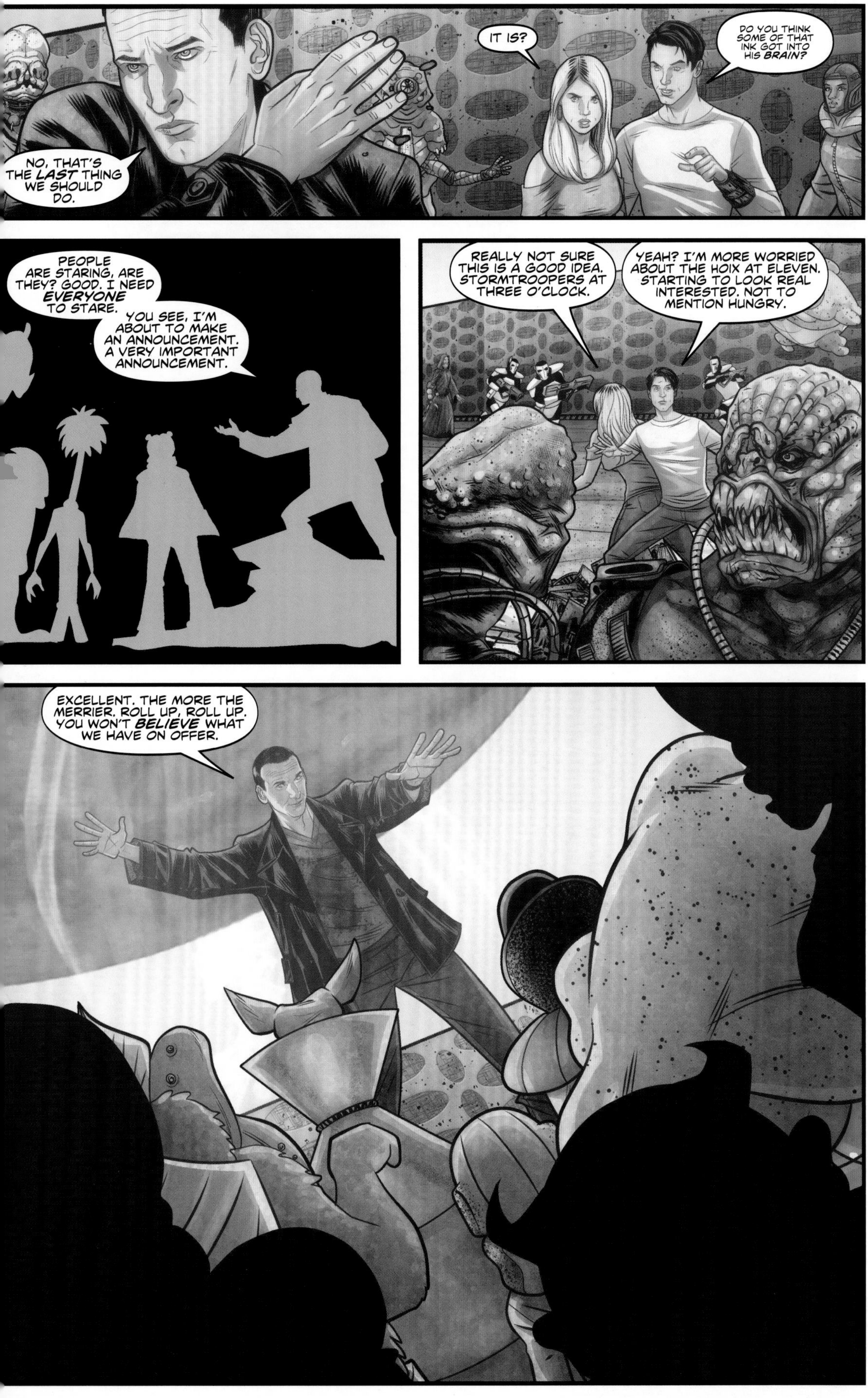
IT IS?
DO YOU THINK SOME OF THAT INK GOT INTO HIS BRAIN?
NO, THAT'S THE LAST THING WE SHOULD DO.
PEOPLE ARE STARING, ARE THEY? GOOD. I NEED EVERYONE TO STARE.
YOU SEE, I'M ABOUT TO MAKE AN ANNOUNCEMENT. A VERY IMPORTANT ANNOUNCEMENT.
REALLY NOT SURE THIS IS A GOOD IDEA. STORMTROOPERS AT THREE O'CLOCK.
YEAH? I'M MORE WORRIED ABOUT THE HOIX AT ELEVEN. STARTING TO LOOK REAL INTERESTED. NOT TO MENTION HUNGRY.
EXCELLENT. THE MORE THE MERRIER. ROLL UP, ROLL UP. YOU WON'T BELIEVE WHAT WE HAVE ON OFFER.

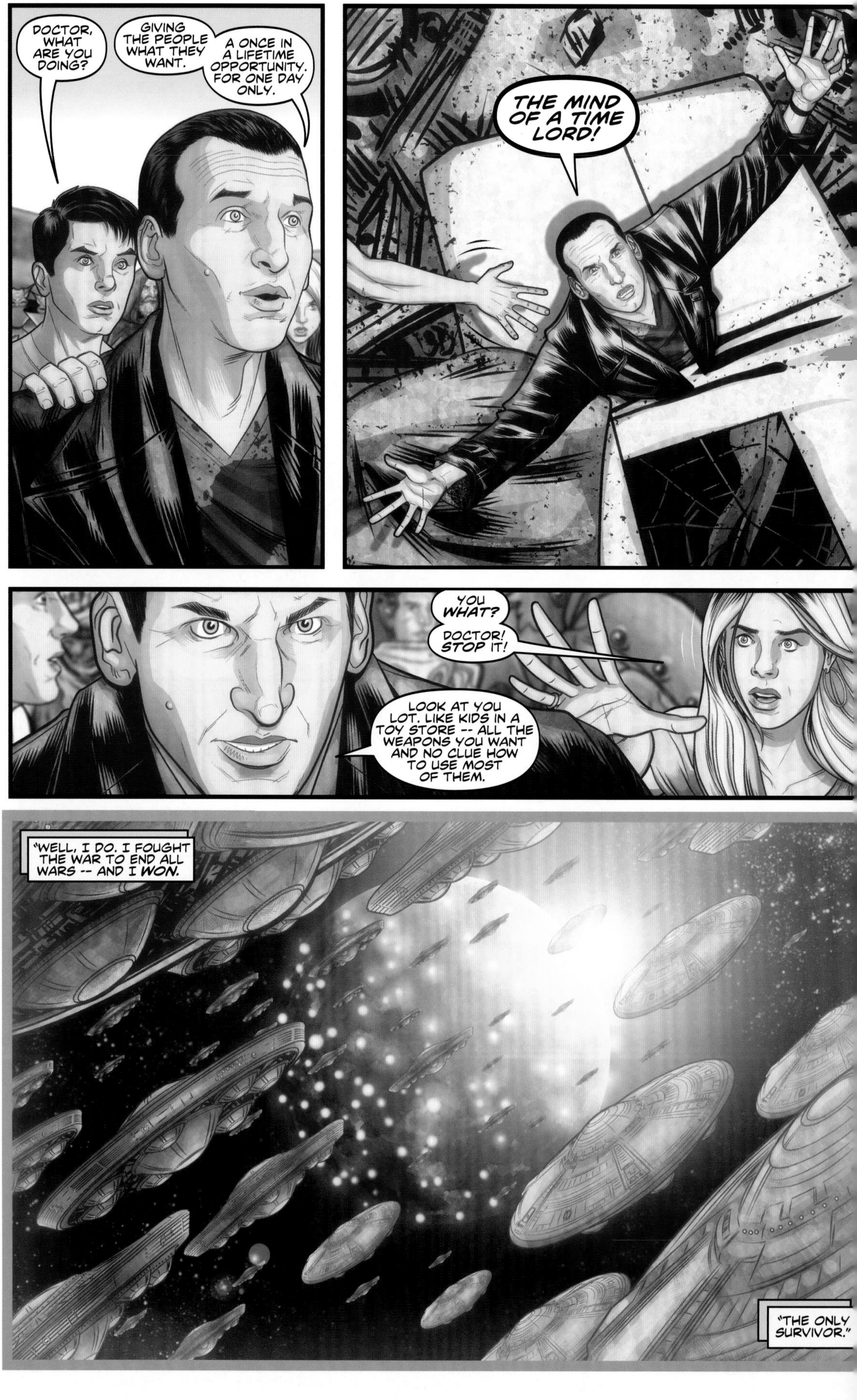
DOCTOR, WHAT ARE YOU DOING?
GIVING THE PEOPLE WHAT THEY WANT.
A ONCE IN A LIFETIME OPPORTUNITY. FOR ONE DAY ONLY.
THE MIND OF A TIME LORD!
YOU WHAT?
DOCTOR! STOP IT!
LOOK AT YOU LOT. LIKE KIDS IN A TOY STORE -- ALL THE WEAPONS YOU WANT AND NO CLUE HOW TO USE MOST OF THEM.
"WELL, I DO. I FOUGHT THE WAR TO END ALL WARS -- AND I WON.
"THE ONLY SURVIVOR."

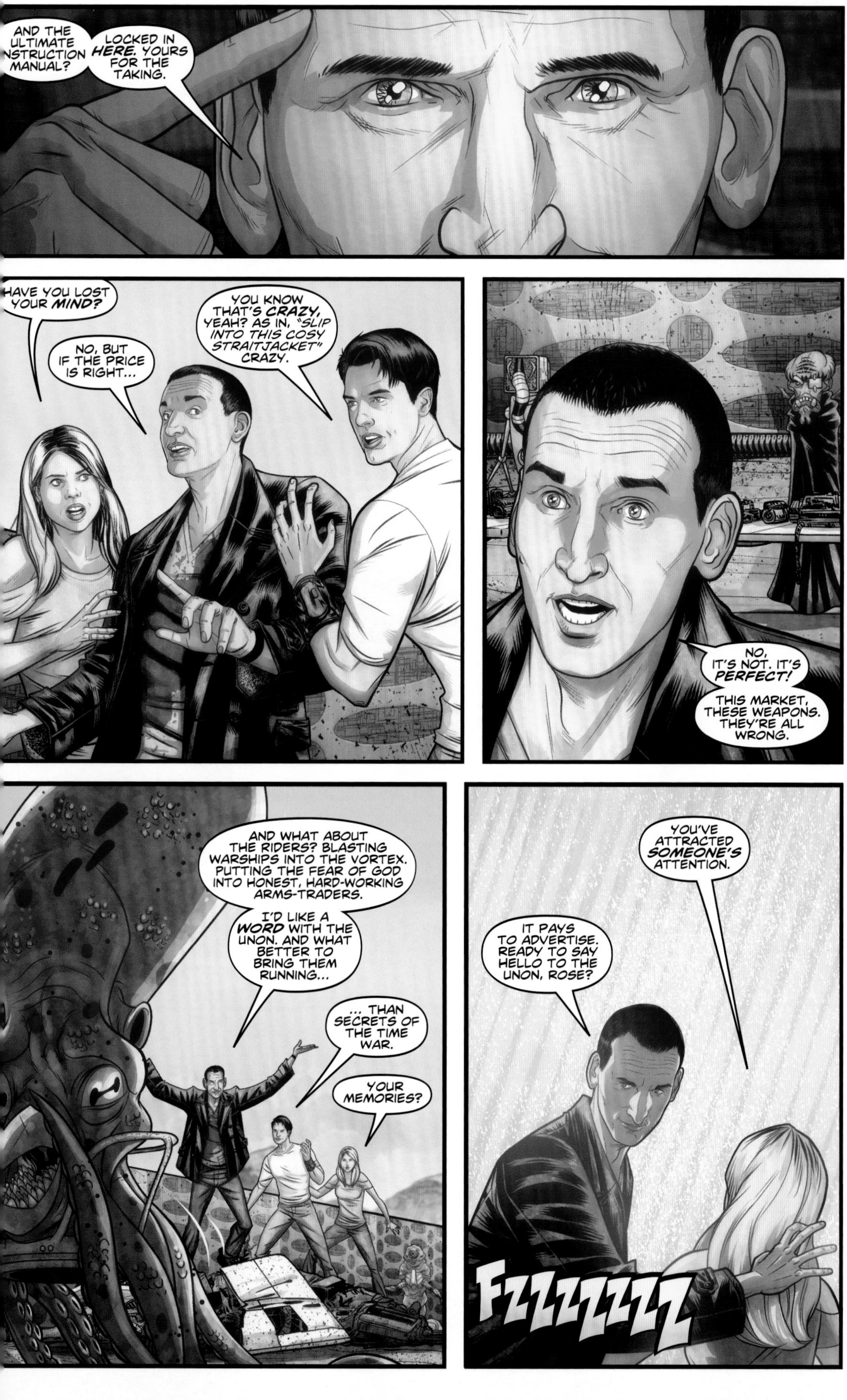

AND THE ULTIMATE NSTRUCTION MANUAL?
LOCKED IN HERE. YOURS FOR THE TAKING.
HAVE YOU LOST YOUR MIND?
NO, BUT IF THE PRICE IS RIGHT...
YOU KNOW THAT'S CRAZY, YEAH? AS IN, "SLIP INTO THIS COSY STRAITJACKET" CRAZY.
NO, IT'S NOT. IT'S PERFECT!
THIS MARKET, THESE WEAPONS. THEY'RE ALL WRONG.
AND WHAT ABOUT THE RIDERS? BLASTING WARSHIPS INTO THE VORTEX. PUTTING THE FEAR OF GOD INTO HONEST, HARD-WORKING ARMS-TRADERS.
I'D LIKE A WORD WITH THE UNON. AND WHAT BETTER TO BRING THEM RUNNING...
... THAN SECRETS OF THE TIME WAR.
YOUR MEMORIES?
YOU'VE ATTRACTED SOMEONE'S ATTENTION.
IT PAYS TO ADVERTISE. READY TO SAY HELLO TO THE UNON, ROSE?
FZZZZZZZ

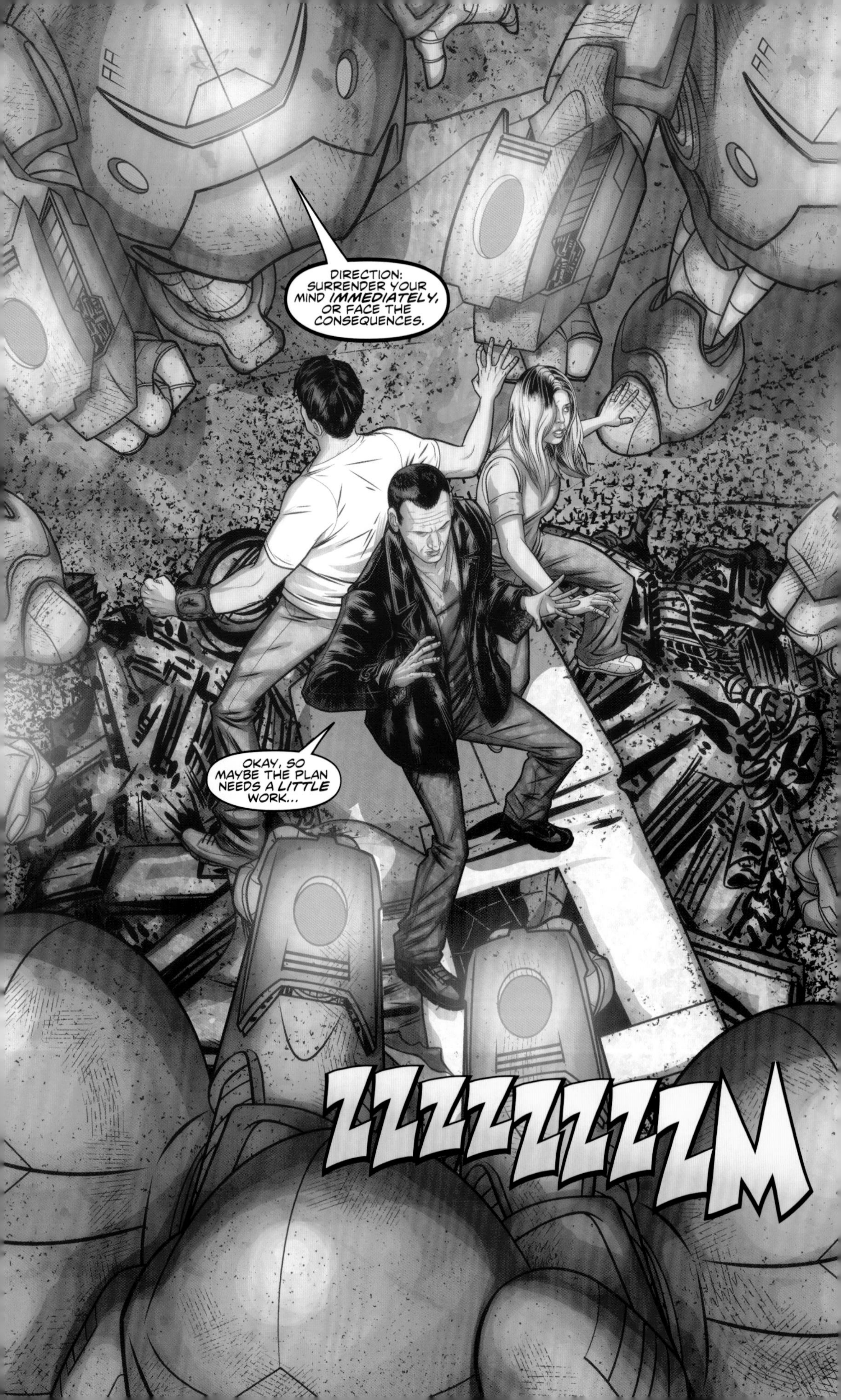
DIRECTION: SURRENDER YOUR MIND *IMMEDIATELY*, OR FACE THE CONSEQUENCES.
OKAY, SO MAYBE THE PLAN NEEDS A *LITTLE* WORK...
ZZZZZZZZZM

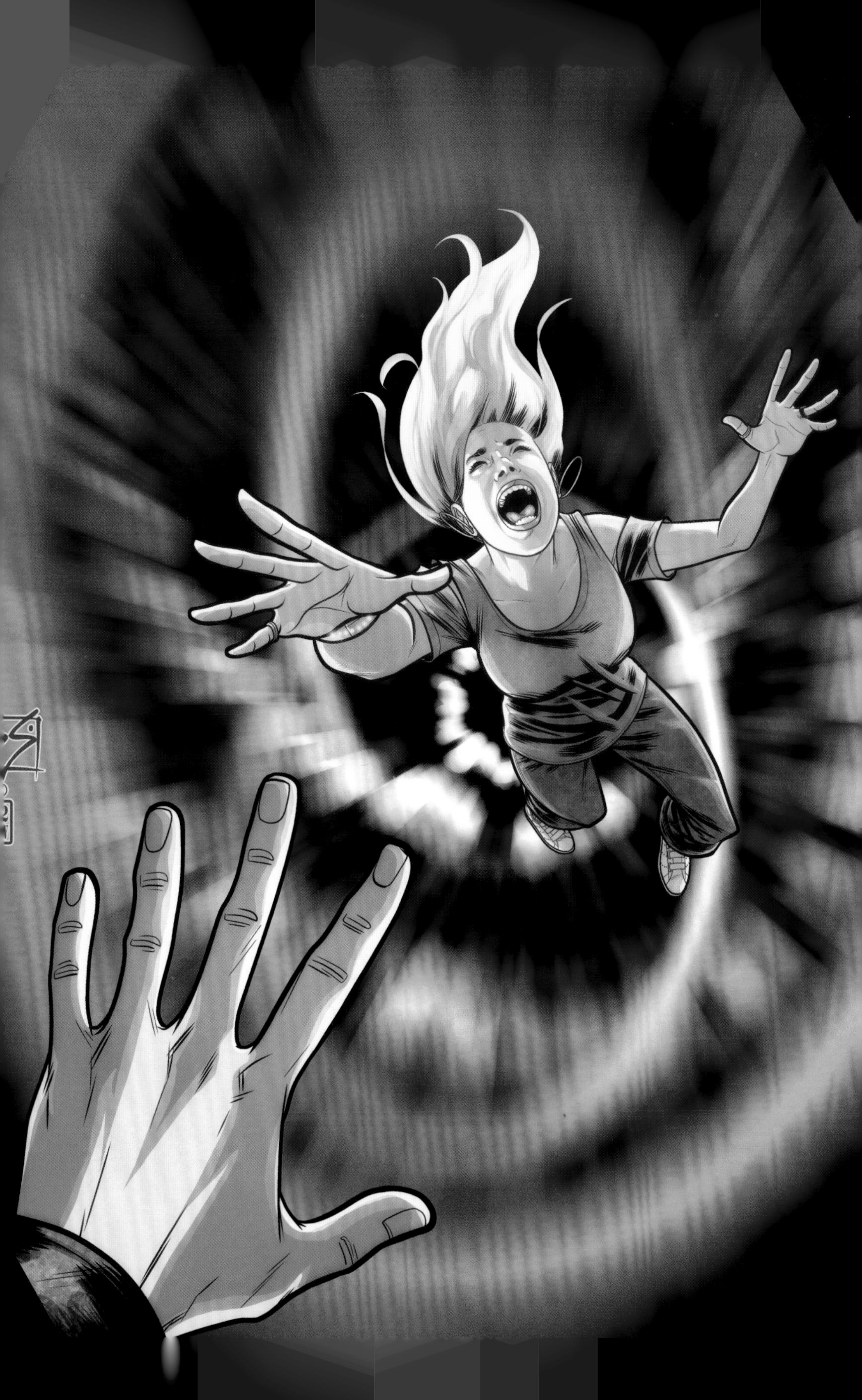

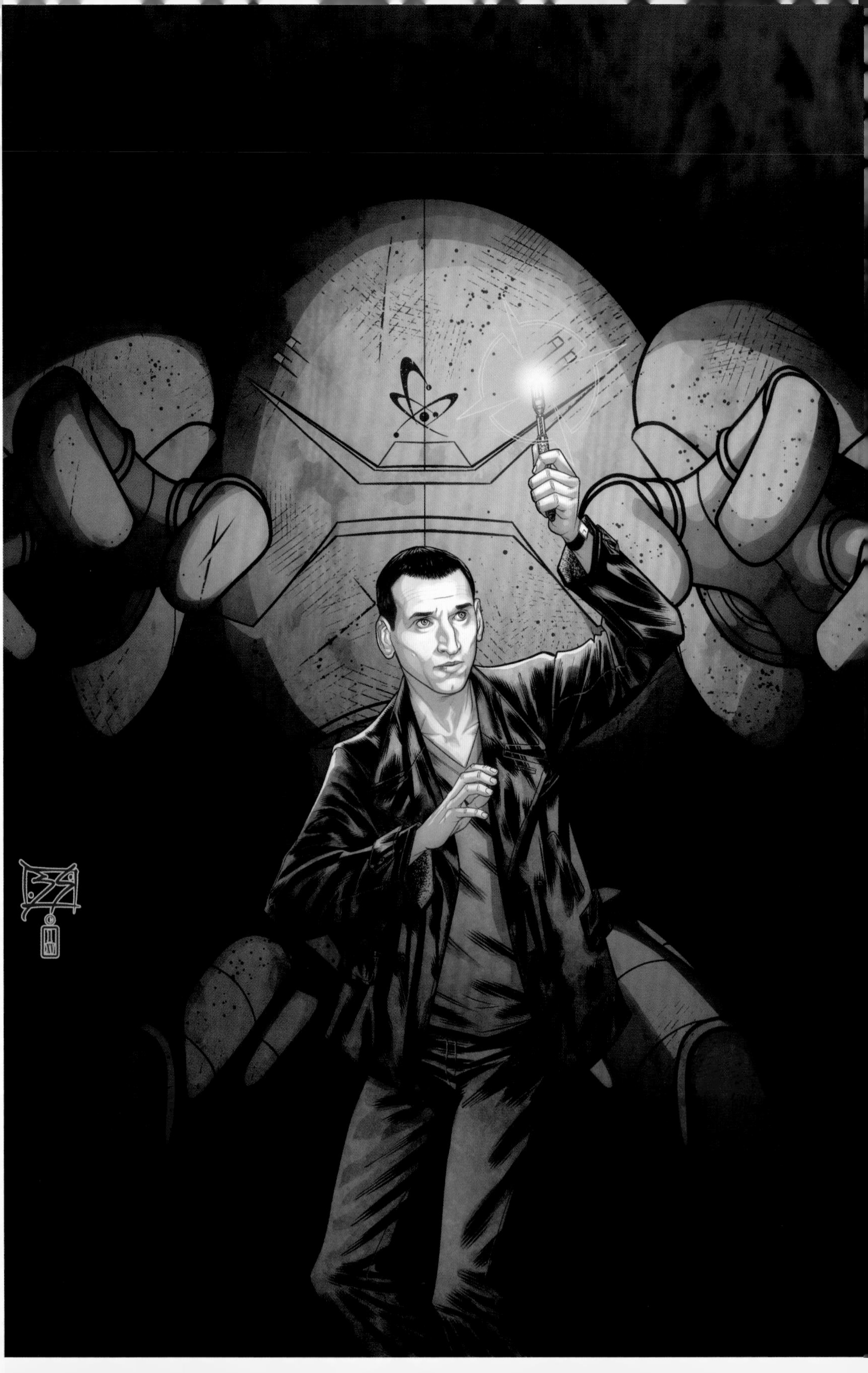

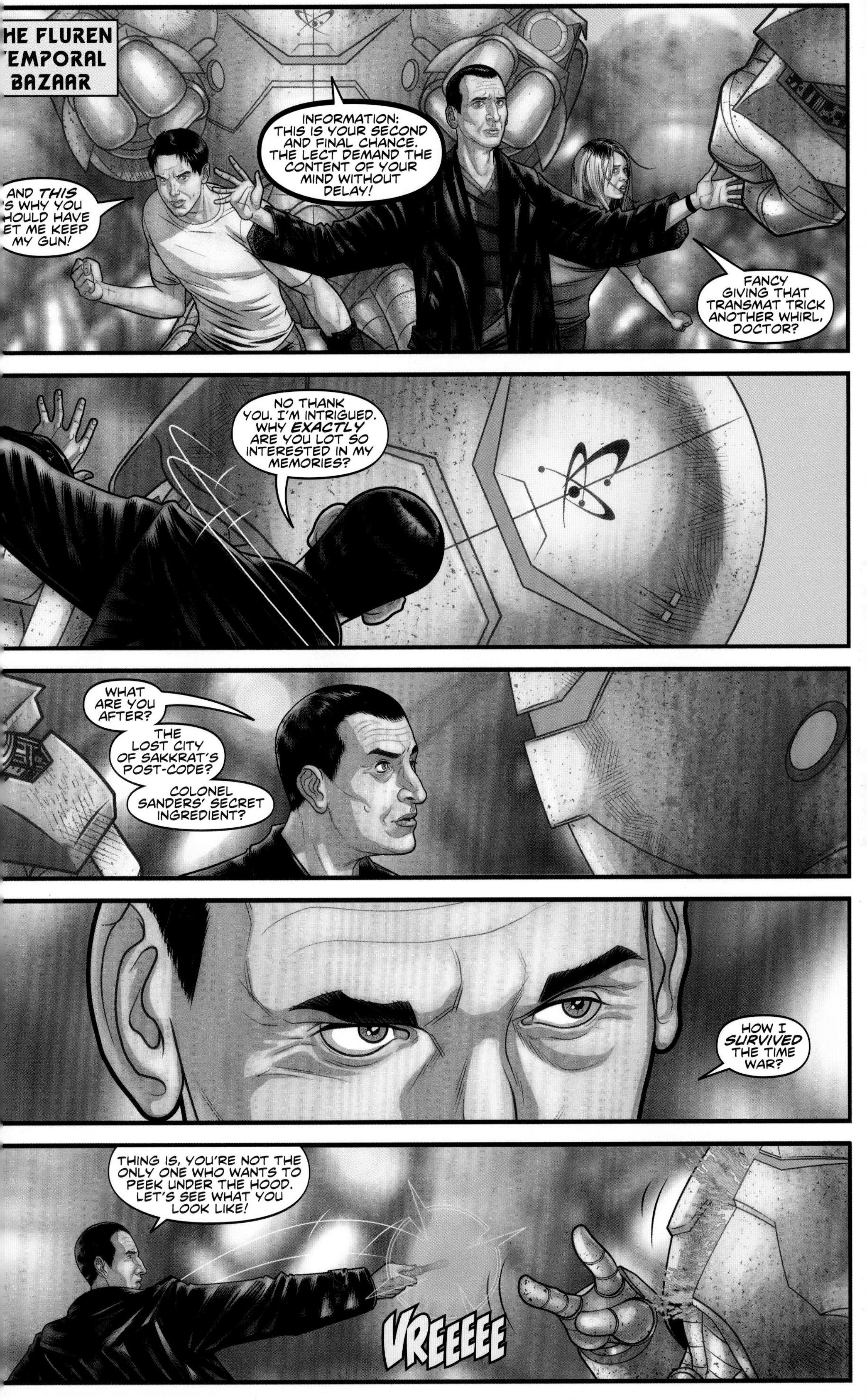
HE FLUREN 'EMPORAL BAZAAR
INFORMATION: THIS IS YOUR SECOND AND FINAL CHANCE. THE LECT DEMAND THE CONTENT OF YOUR MIND WITHOUT DELAY!
AND THIS 'S WHY YOU HOULD HAVE ET ME KEEP MY GUN!
FANCY GIVING THAT TRANSMAT TRICK ANOTHER WHIRL, DOCTOR?
NO THANK YOU. I'M INTRIGUED. WHY EXACTLY ARE YOU LOT SO INTERESTED IN MY MEMORIES?
WHAT ARE YOU AFTER?
THE LOST CITY OF SAKKRAT'S POST-CODE?
COLONEL SANDERS' SECRET INGREDIENT?
HOW I SURVIVED THE TIME WAR?
THING IS, YOU'RE NOT THE ONLY ONE WHO WANTS TO PEEK UNDER THE HOOD. LET'S SEE WHAT YOU LOOK LIKE!
VREEEEE

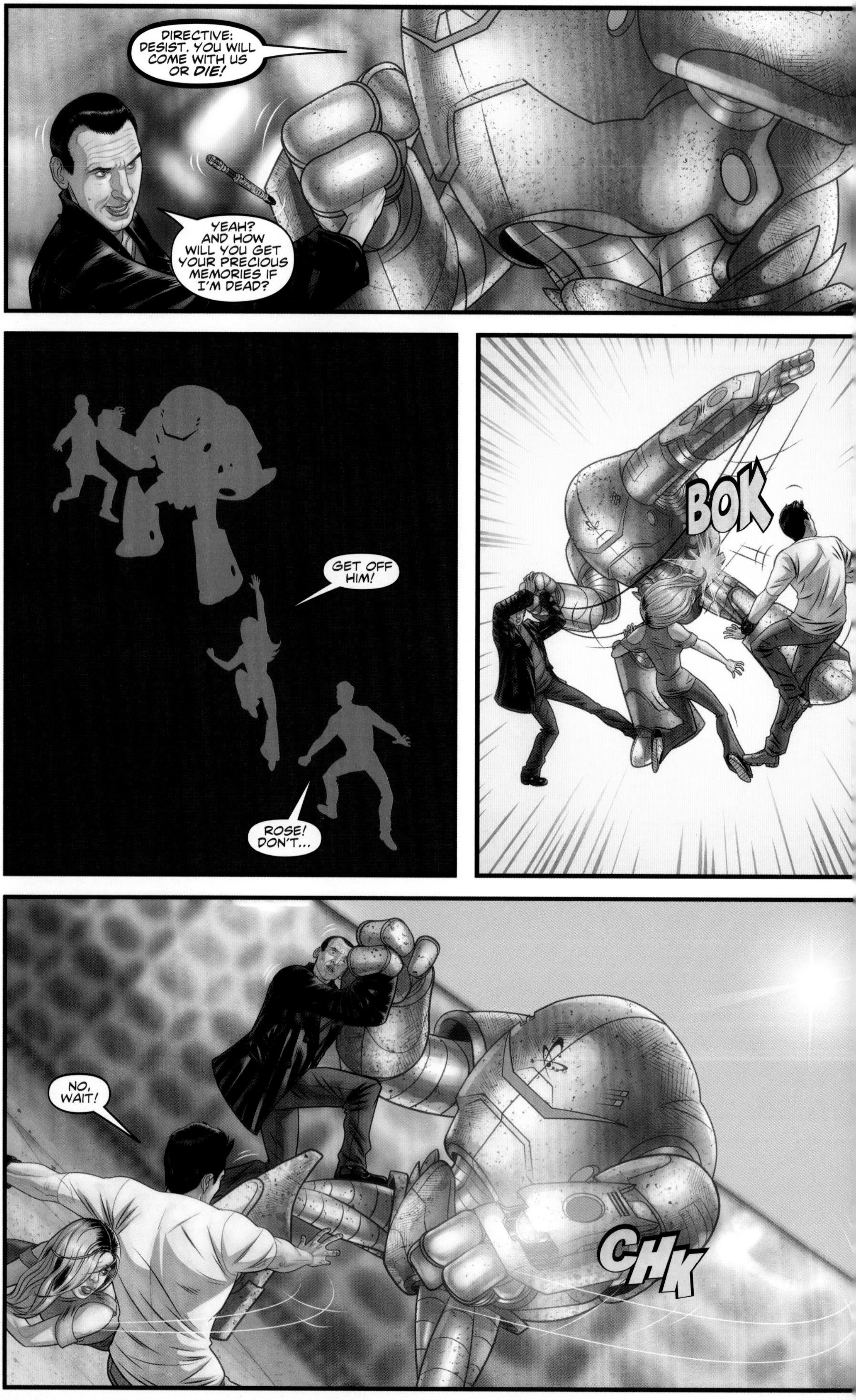
DIRECTIVE: DESIST. YOU WILL COME WITH US OR *DIE!*
YEAH? AND HOW WILL YOU GET YOUR PRECIOUS MEMORIES IF I'M DEAD?
GET OFF HIM!
ROSE! DON'T...
BOK
NO, WAIT!
CHK

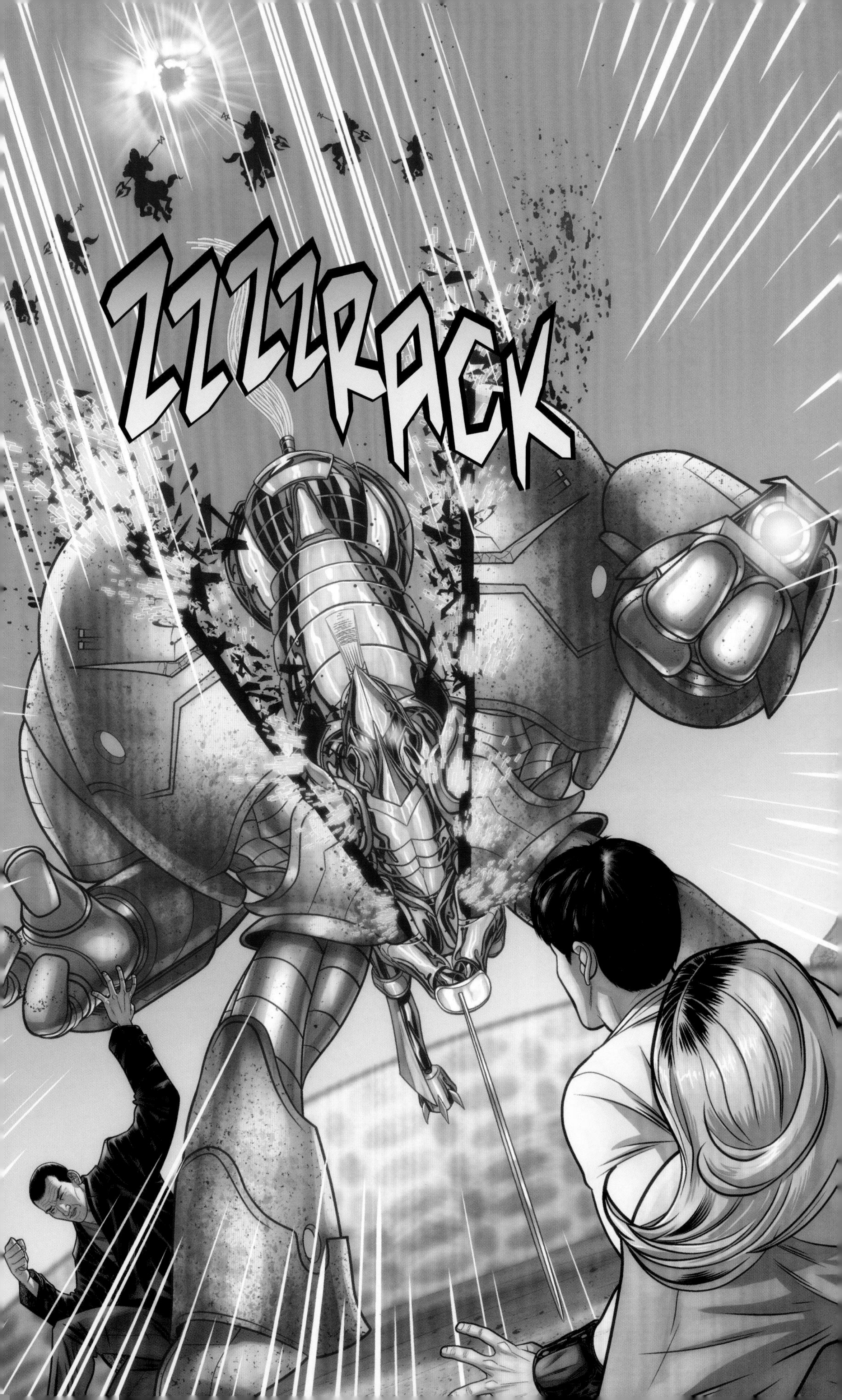
ZZZZRACK

LOOKS LIKE YOU GOT YOUR WISH. GOOD OLD UNON, EH?

BETTER LATE THAN NEVER. THEY *REALLY* DON'T LIKE THE LECT, DO THEY?

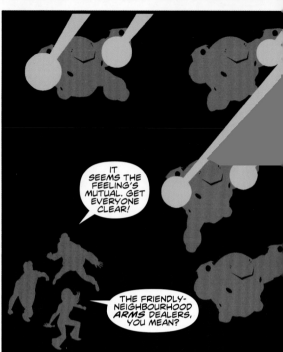

IT SEEMS THE FEELING'S MUTUAL. GET EVERYONE CLEAR!

THE FRIENDLY-NEIGHBOURHOOD *ARMS* DEALERS, YOU MEAN?

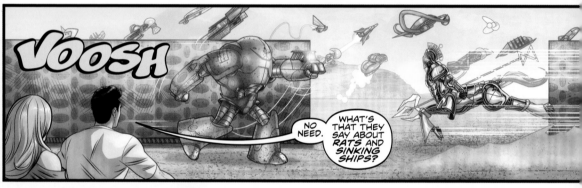

VOOSH

NO NEED.

WHAT'S THAT THEY SAY ABOUT *RATS* AND *SINKING SHIPS?*

VOOM

WEAPONS NOT SO CLEVER NOW *THE RATS* ARE THE ONES UNDER ATTACK!

IF YOU'VE *ANY* SENSE IN THAT BONY SKULL OF YOURS, YOU'LL FOLLOW THEIR EXAMPLE. GET OUT OF HERE BEFORE THE *EMERGENCY PROTOCOL* IS TRIGGERED.

HEY, *WATCH IT,* INKY! DON'T BARGE WHAT YOU CAN'T AFFORD!

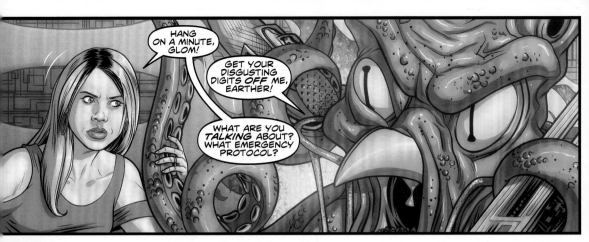

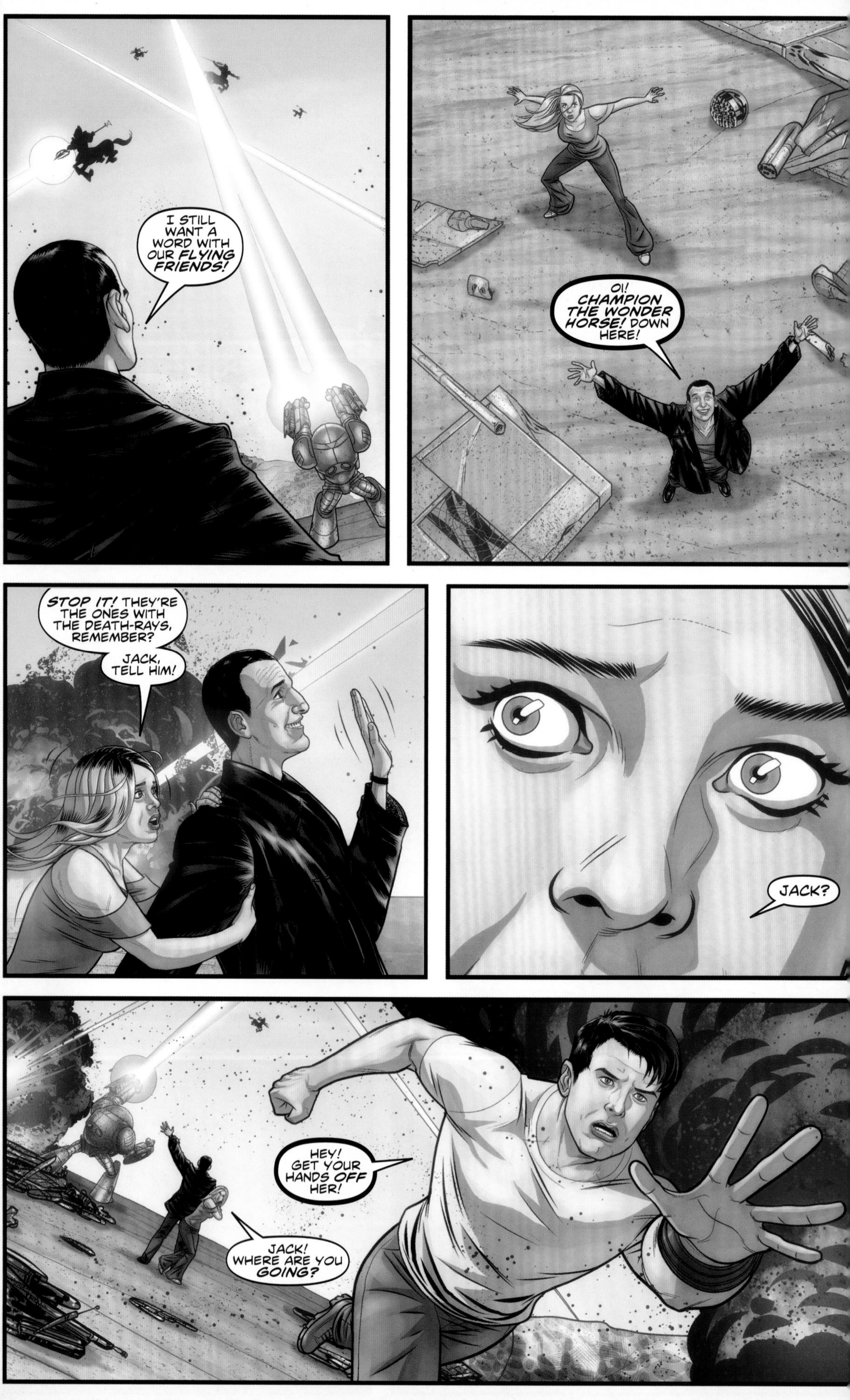
I STILL WANT A WORD WITH OUR FLYING FRIENDS!
OI! CHAMPION THE WONDER HORSE! DOWN HERE!
STOP IT! THEY'RE THE ONES WITH THE DEATH-RAYS, REMEMBER?
JACK, TELL HIM!
JACK?
HEY! GET YOUR HANDS OFF HER!
JACK! WHERE ARE YOU GOING?

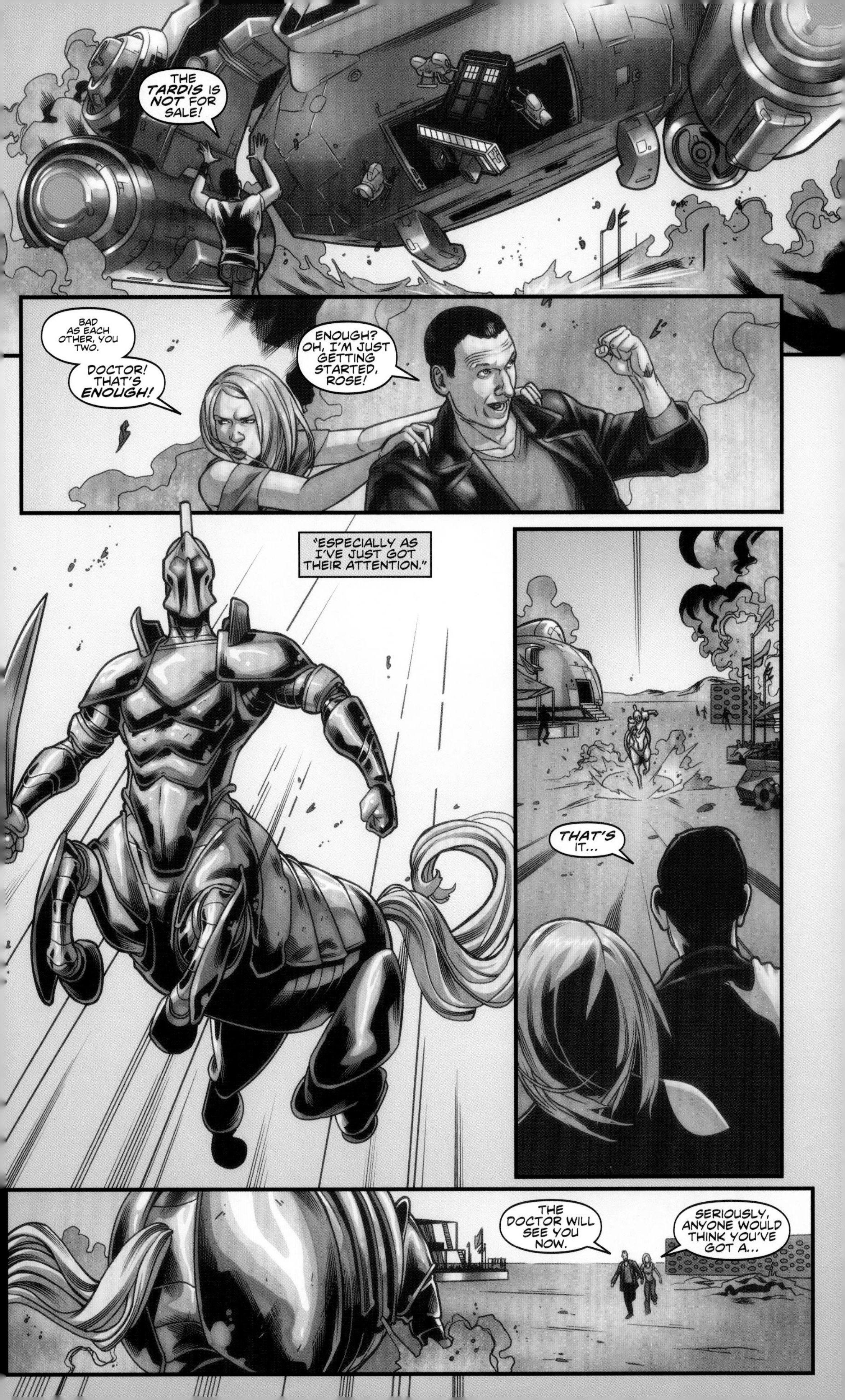
THE TARDIS IS NOT FOR SALE!
BAD AS EACH OTHER, YOU TWO.
DOCTOR! THAT'S ENOUGH!
ENOUGH? OH, I'M JUST GETTING STARTED, ROSE!
"ESPECIALLY AS I'VE JUST GOT THEIR ATTENTION."
THAT'S IT...
THE DOCTOR WILL SEE YOU NOW.
SERIOUSLY, ANYONE WOULD THINK YOU'VE GOT A...

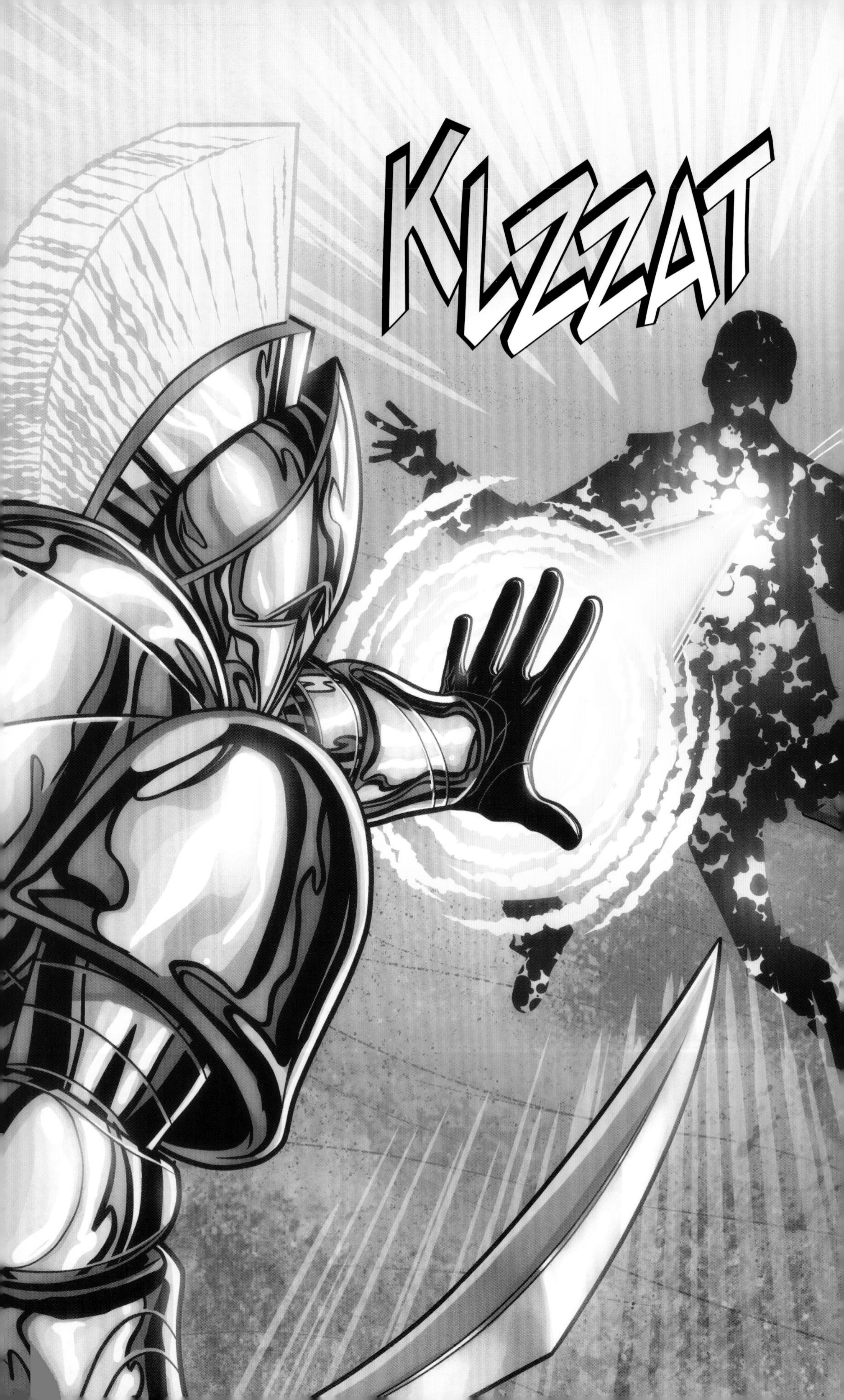
KLZZAT

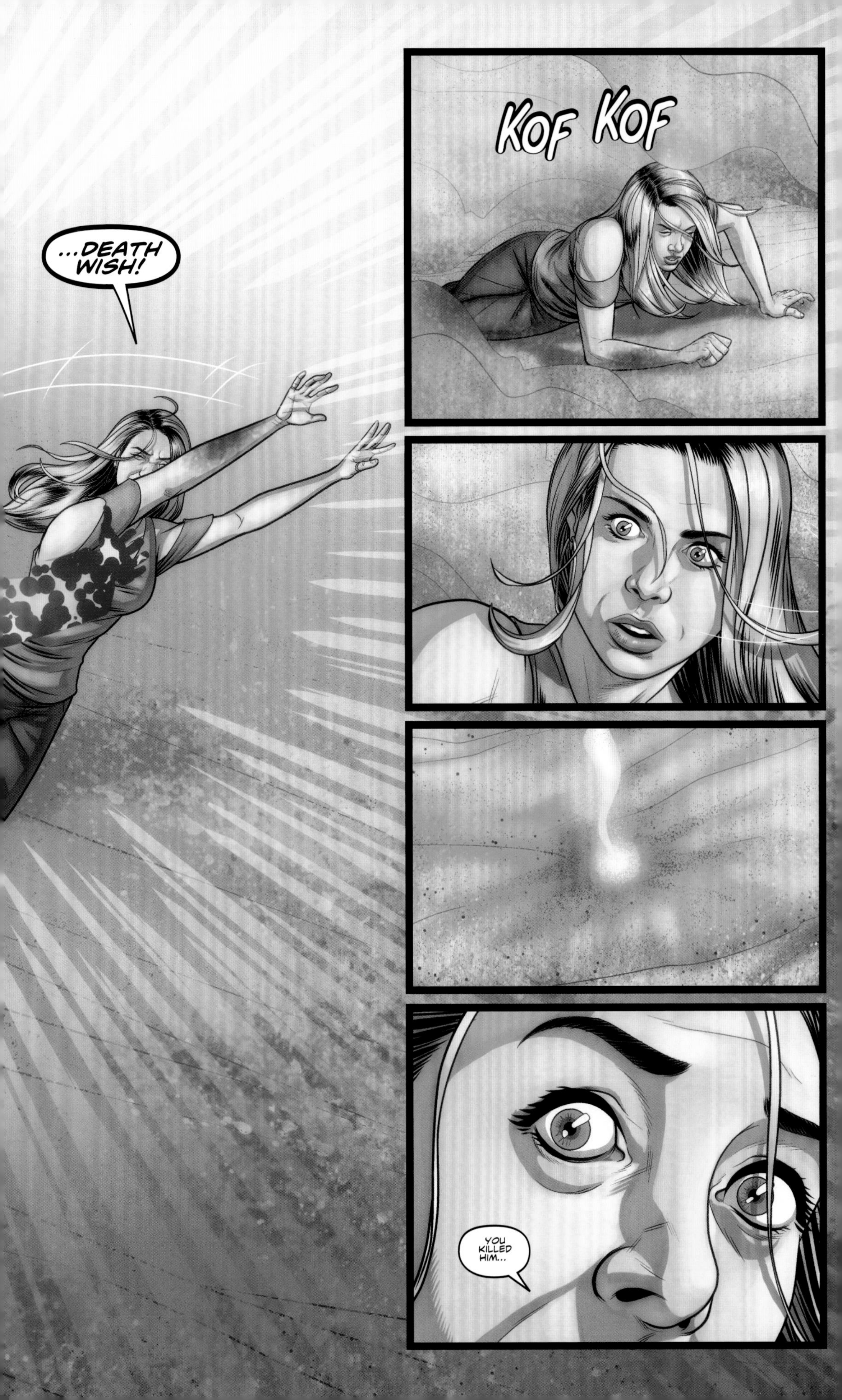
...DEATH WISH!
KOF KOF
YOU KILLED HIM...

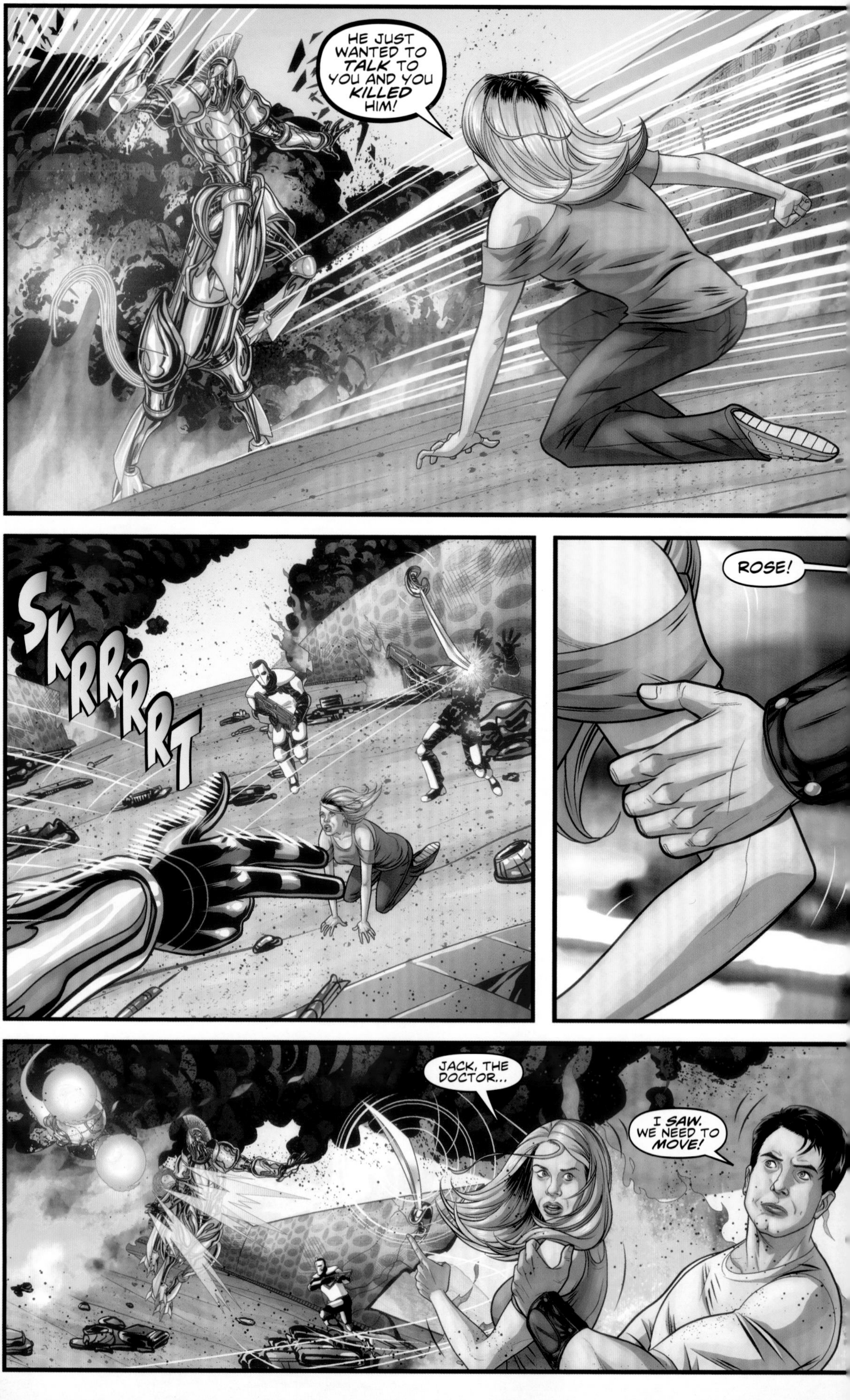
HE JUST WANTED TO TALK TO YOU AND YOU KILLED HIM!
SKRRRRRT
ROSE!
JACK, THE DOCTOR...
I SAW. WE NEED TO MOVE!

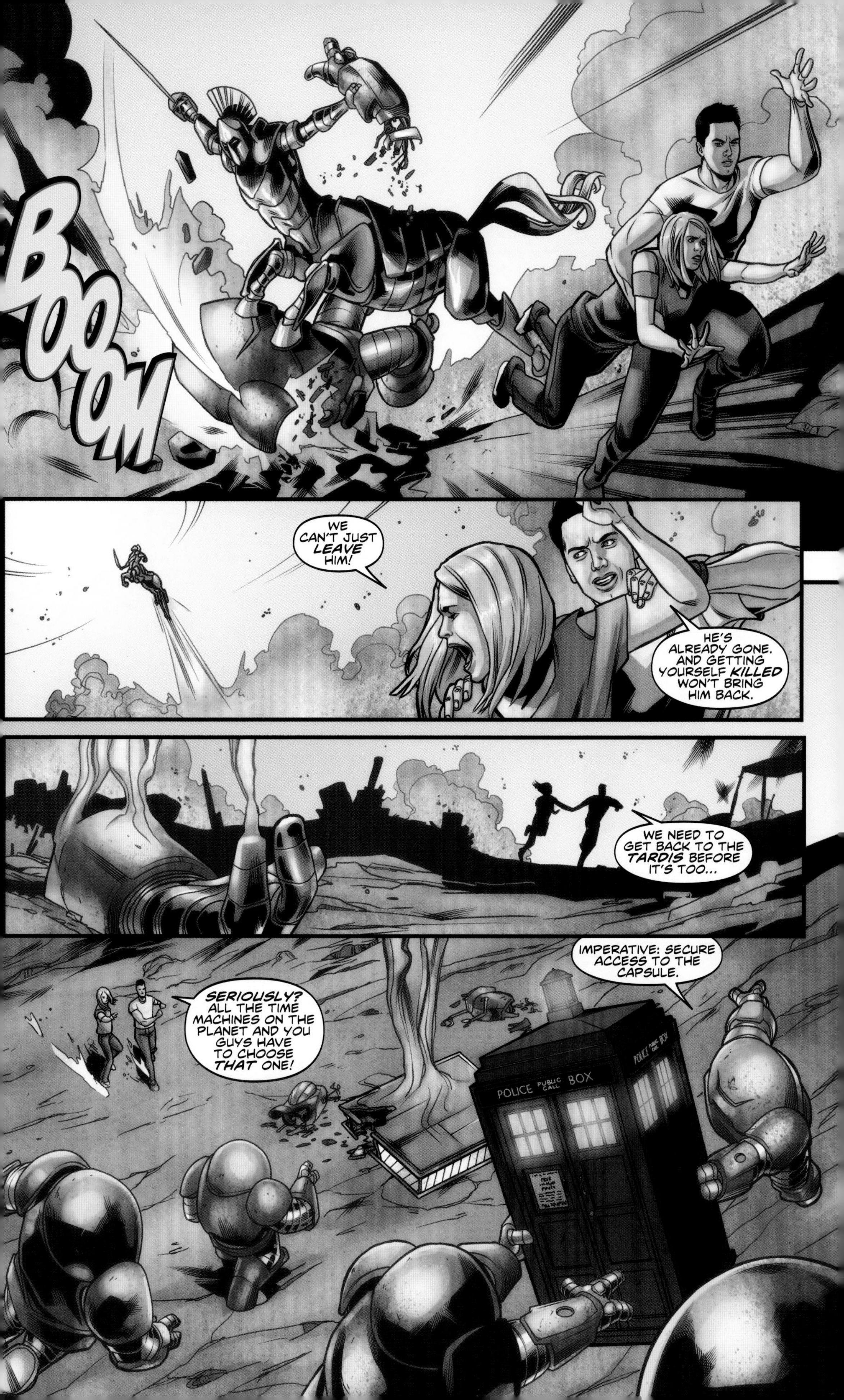
BOOOM
WE CAN'T JUST *LEAVE* HIM!
HE'S ALREADY GONE. AND GETTING YOURSELF *KILLED* WON'T BRING HIM BACK.
WE NEED TO GET BACK TO THE *TARDIS* BEFORE IT'S TOO...
IMPERATIVE: SECURE ACCESS TO THE CAPSULE.
SERIOUSLY? ALL THE TIME MACHINES ON THE PLANET AND YOU GUYS HAVE TO CHOOSE *THAT* ONE!
POLICE PUBLIC CALL BOX

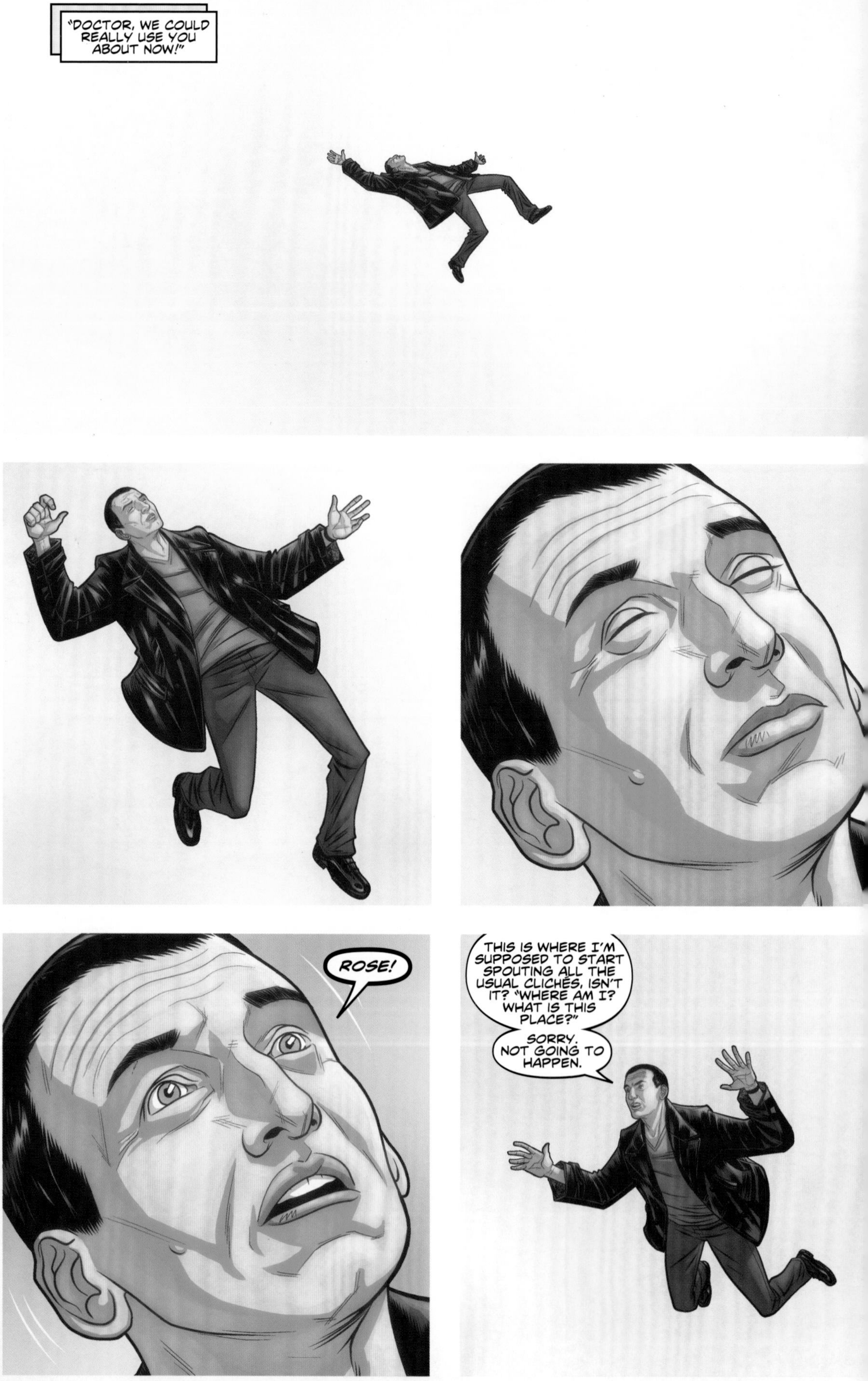
"DOCTOR, WE COULD REALLY USE YOU ABOUT NOW!"
ROSE!
THIS IS WHERE I'M SUPPOSED TO START SPOUTING ALL THE USUAL CLICHÉS, ISN'T IT? "WHERE AM I? WHAT IS THIS PLACE?"
SORRY. NOT GOING TO HAPPEN.

AND YOU MIGHT AS WELL SHOW YOURSELF. TIME-TOT HIDE AND SEEK CHAMPION, ME. FORTY-TWO-YEARS ON THE TROT. NO HIDING PLACE WAS SAFE. USED TO DRIVE THE RANI *NUTS.*

THERE YOU ARE. IT'S *RUDE,* YOU KNOW? DUMPING SOMEONE IN A SUB-DIMENSIONAL VOID. THAT *IS* WHERE WE ARE, ISN'T IT?

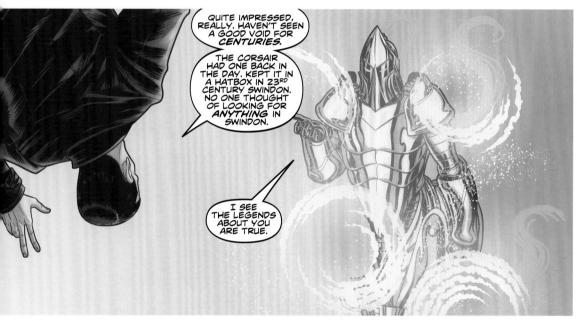

QUITE IMPRESSED, REALLY. HAVEN'T SEEN A GOOD VOID FOR *CENTURIES.*

THE CORSAIR HAD ONE BACK IN THE DAY. KEPT IT IN A HATBOX IN 23RD CENTURY SWINDON. NO ONE THOUGHT OF LOOKING FOR *ANYTHING* IN SWINDON.

I SEE THE LEGENDS ABOUT YOU ARE TRUE.

LEGENDS? GOT TO LOVE A GOOD LEGEND. GO ON THEN -- WHAT DO THEY SAY?

PLEASE DON'T TELL ME THEY MENTION THE EARS.

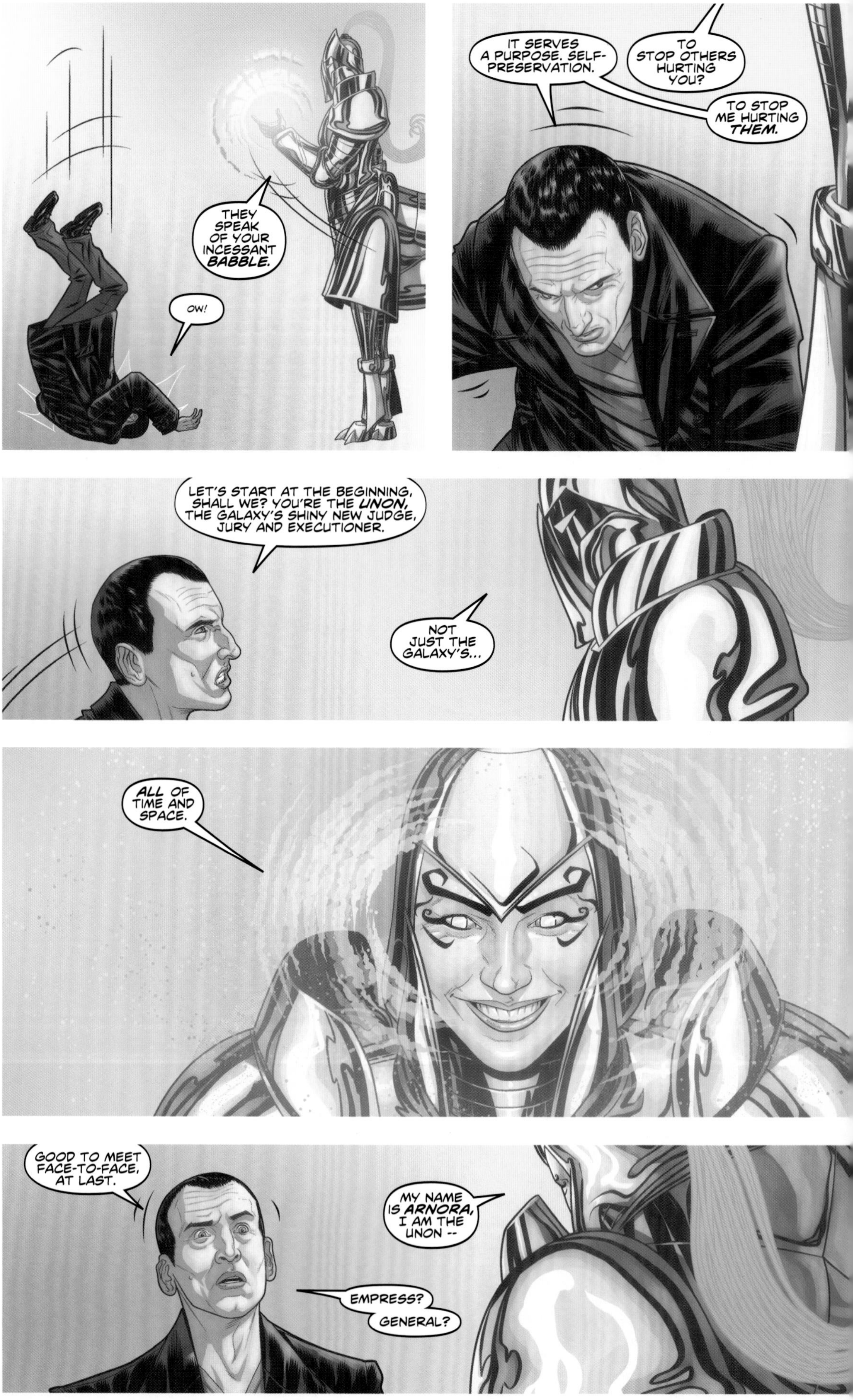
THEY SPEAK OF YOUR INCESSANT ***BABBLE.***
OW!
IT SERVES A PURPOSE. SELF-PRESERVATION.
TO STOP OTHERS HURTING YOU?
TO STOP ME HURTING ***THEM.***
LET'S START AT THE BEGINNING, SHALL WE? YOU'RE THE ***UNON,*** THE GALAXY'S SHINY NEW JUDGE, JURY AND EXECUTIONER.
NOT JUST THE GALAXY'S...
ALL OF TIME AND SPACE.
GOOD TO MEET FACE-TO-FACE, AT LAST.
MY NAME IS ***ARNORA,*** I AM THE UNON --
EMPRESS?
GENERAL?

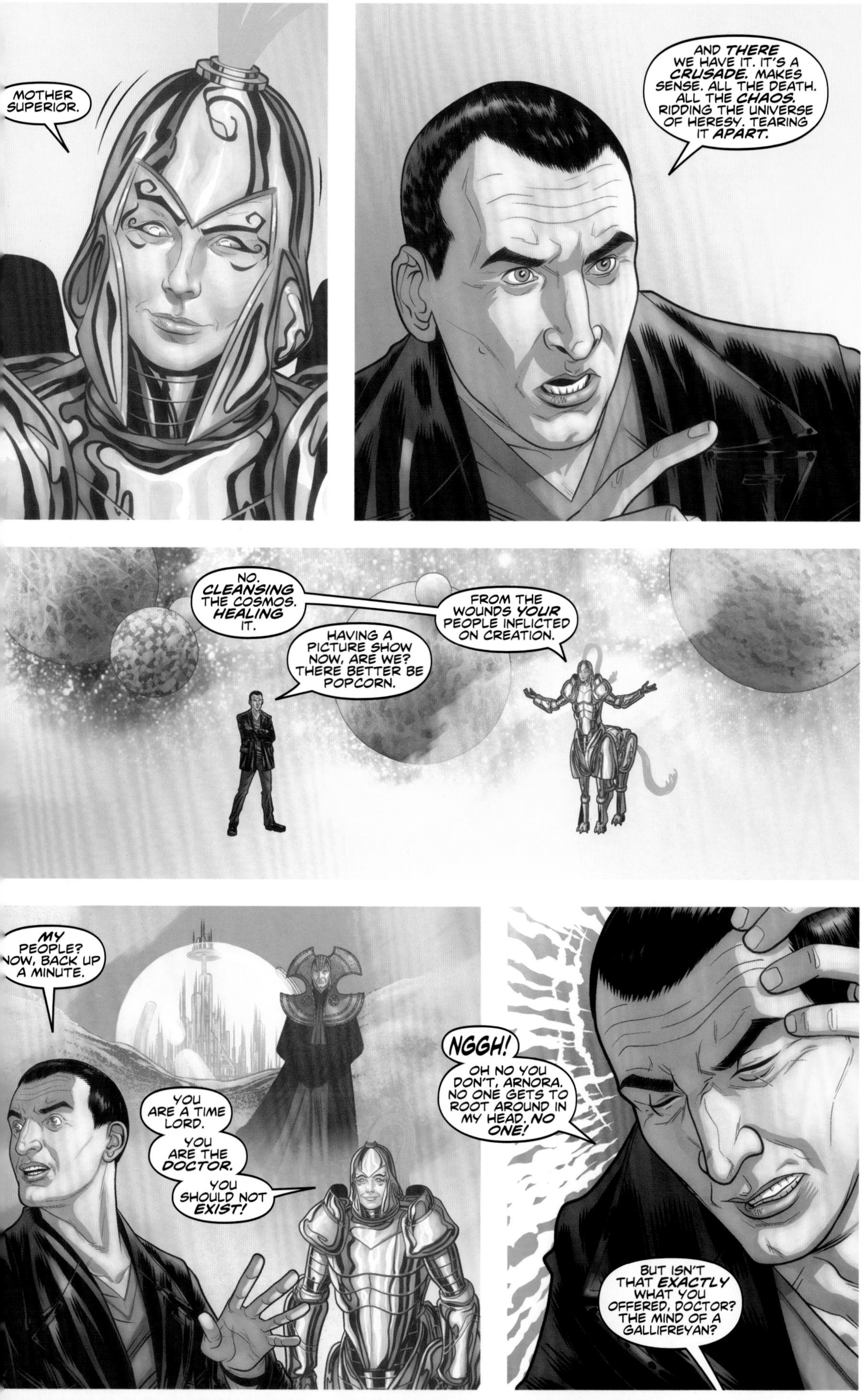
MOTHER SUPERIOR.
AND *THERE* WE HAVE IT. IT'S A *CRUSADE.* MAKES SENSE. ALL THE DEATH. ALL THE *CHAOS.* RIDDING THE UNIVERSE OF HERESY. TEARING IT *APART.*
NO. *CLEANSING* THE COSMOS. *HEALING* IT.
FROM THE WOUNDS *YOUR* PEOPLE INFLICTED ON CREATION.
HAVING A PICTURE SHOW NOW, ARE WE? THERE BETTER BE POPCORN.
MY PEOPLE? NOW, BACK UP A MINUTE.
YOU ARE A TIME LORD.
YOU ARE THE *DOCTOR*.
YOU SHOULD NOT *EXIST!*
NGGH!
OH NO YOU DON'T, ARNORA. NO ONE GETS TO ROOT AROUND IN MY HEAD. *NO ONE!*
BUT ISN'T THAT *EXACTLY* WHAT YOU OFFERED, DOCTOR? THE MIND OF A GALLIFREYAN?

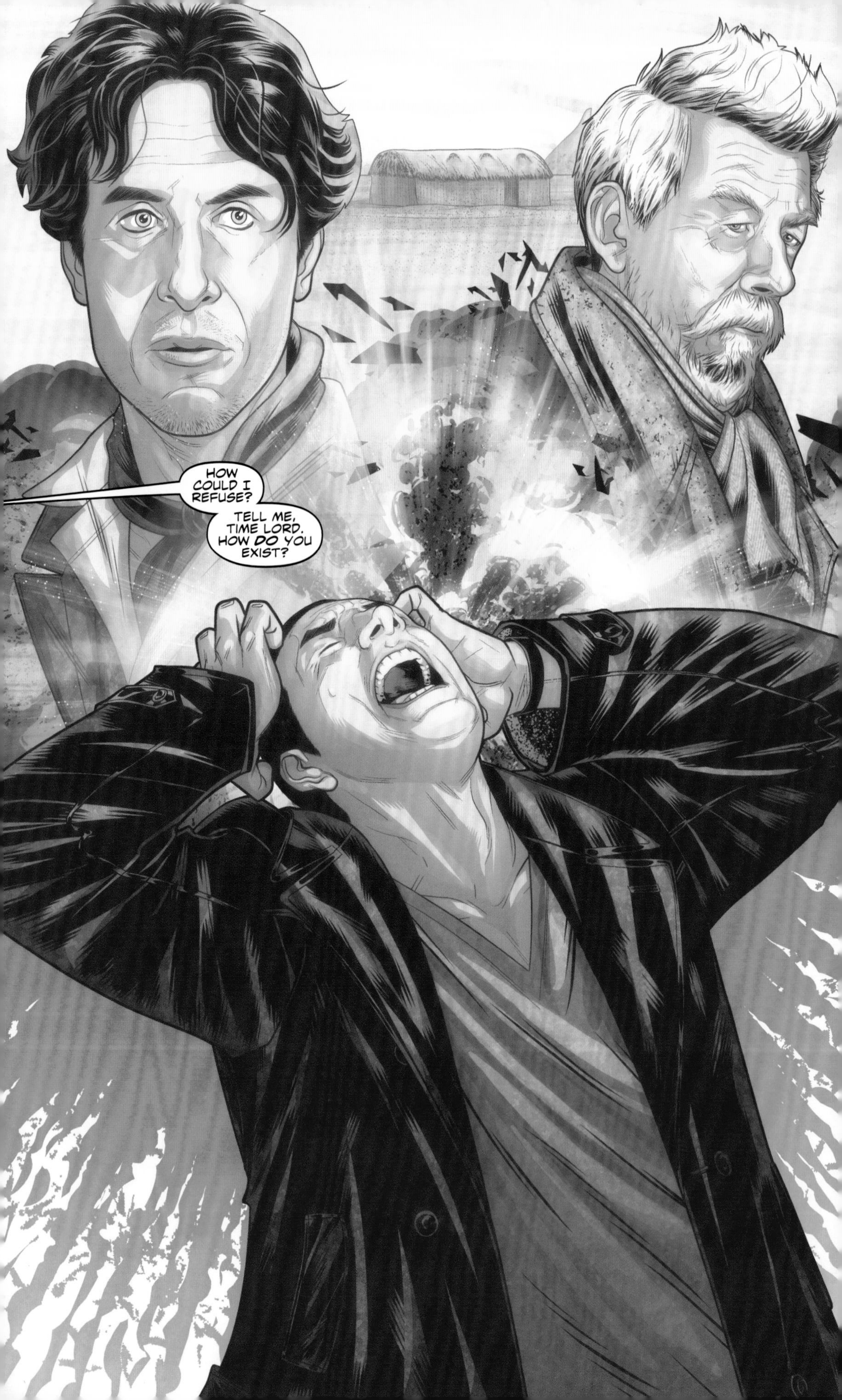
HOW COULD I REFUSE?
TELL ME, TIME LORD. HOW *DO* YOU EXIST?

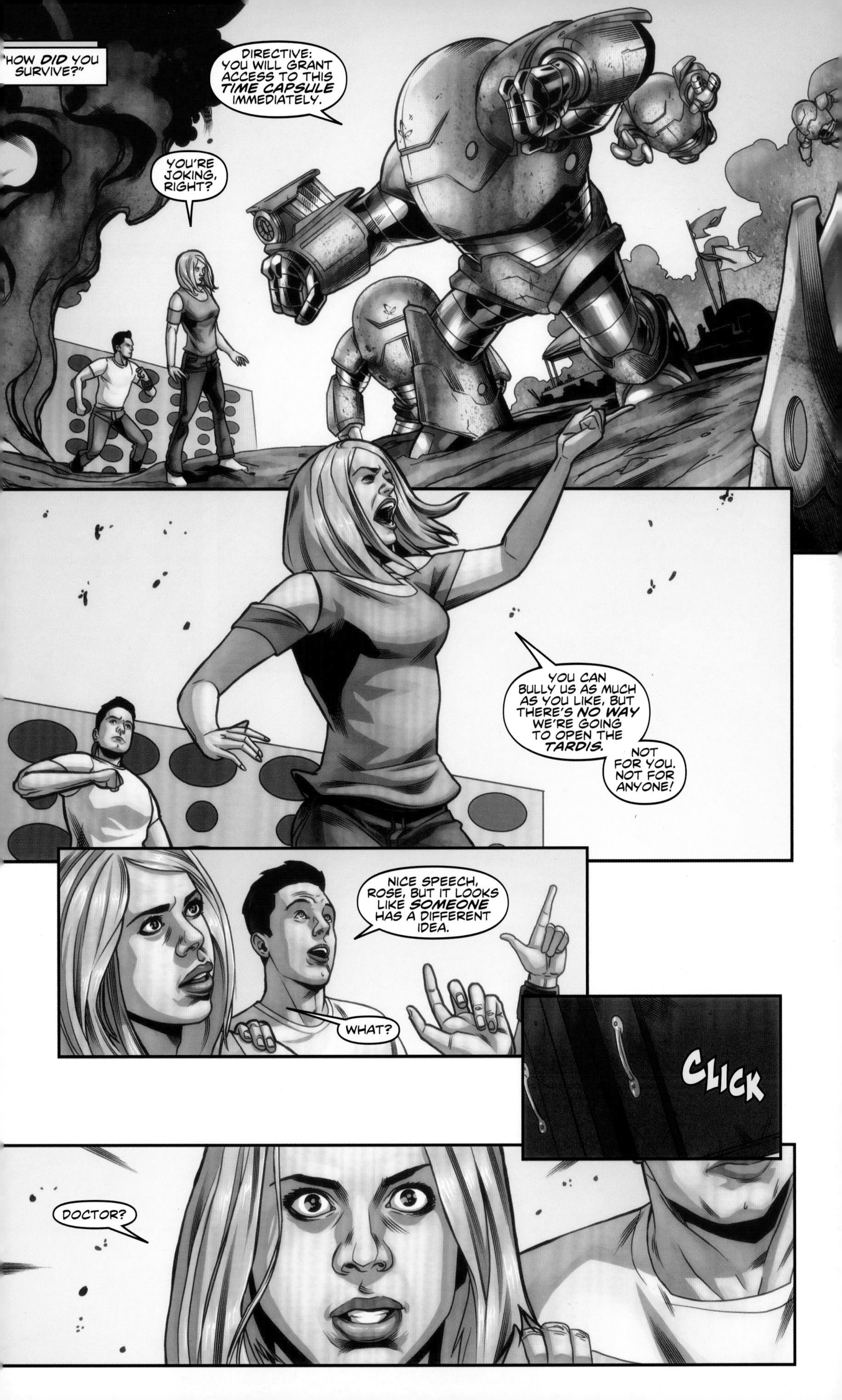
"HOW DID YOU SURVIVE?"
DIRECTIVE: YOU WILL GRANT ACCESS TO THIS TIME CAPSULE IMMEDIATELY.
YOU'RE JOKING, RIGHT?
YOU CAN BULLY US AS MUCH AS YOU LIKE, BUT THERE'S NO WAY WE'RE GOING TO OPEN THE TARDIS.
NOT FOR YOU. NOT FOR ANYONE!
NICE SPEECH, ROSE, BUT IT LOOKS LIKE SOMEONE HAS A DIFFERENT IDEA.
WHAT?
CLICK
DOCTOR?

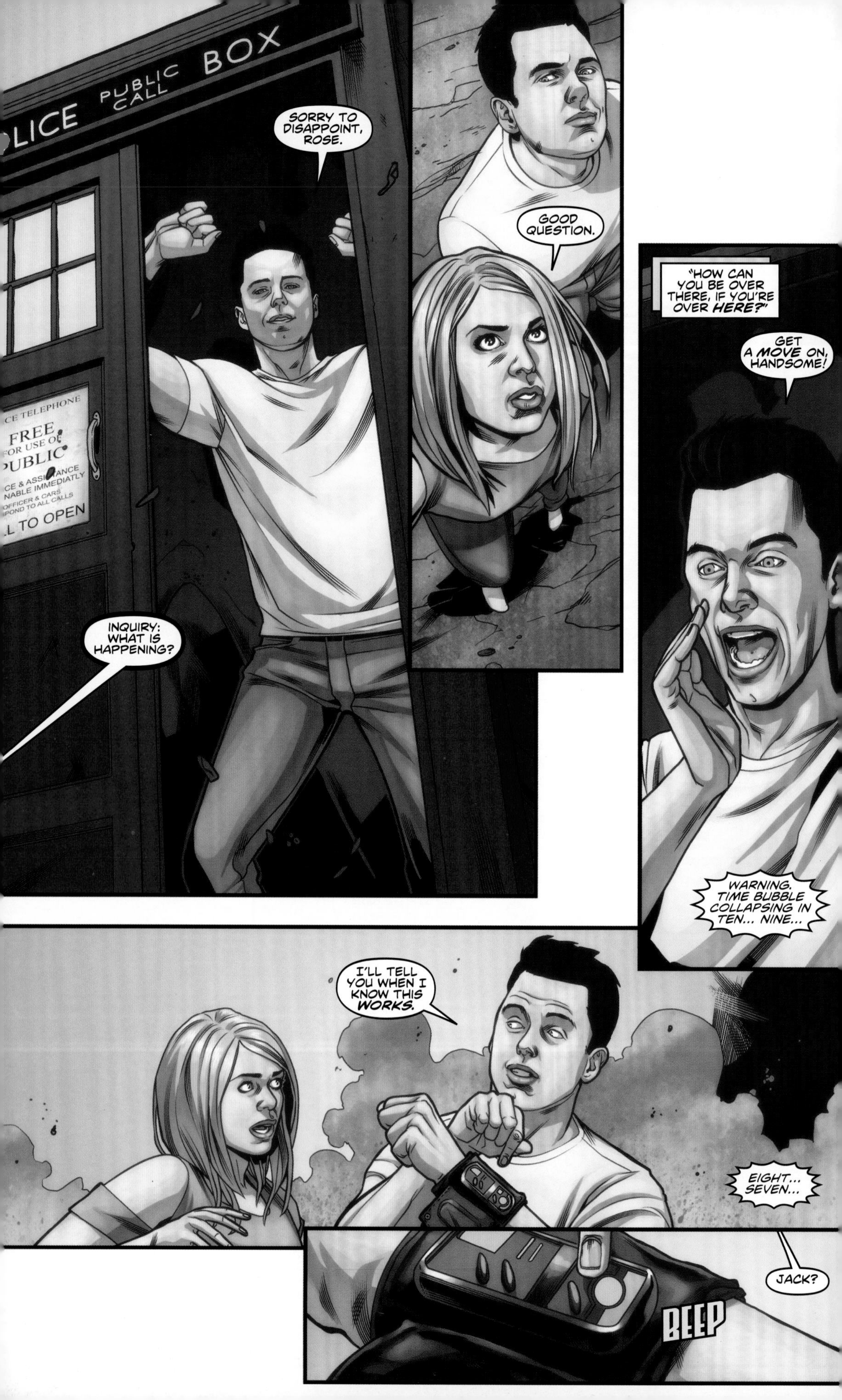
POLICE PUBLIC CALL BOX
POLICE TELEPHONE FREE FOR USE OF PUBLIC
PULL TO OPEN
SORRY TO DISAPPOINT, ROSE.
GOOD QUESTION.
"HOW CAN YOU BE OVER THERE, IF YOU'RE OVER HERE?"
GET A MOVE ON, HANDSOME!
INQUIRY: WHAT IS HAPPENING?
WARNING. TIME BUBBLE COLLAPSING IN TEN... NINE...
I'LL TELL YOU WHEN I KNOW THIS WORKS.
EIGHT... SEVEN...
JACK?
BEEP

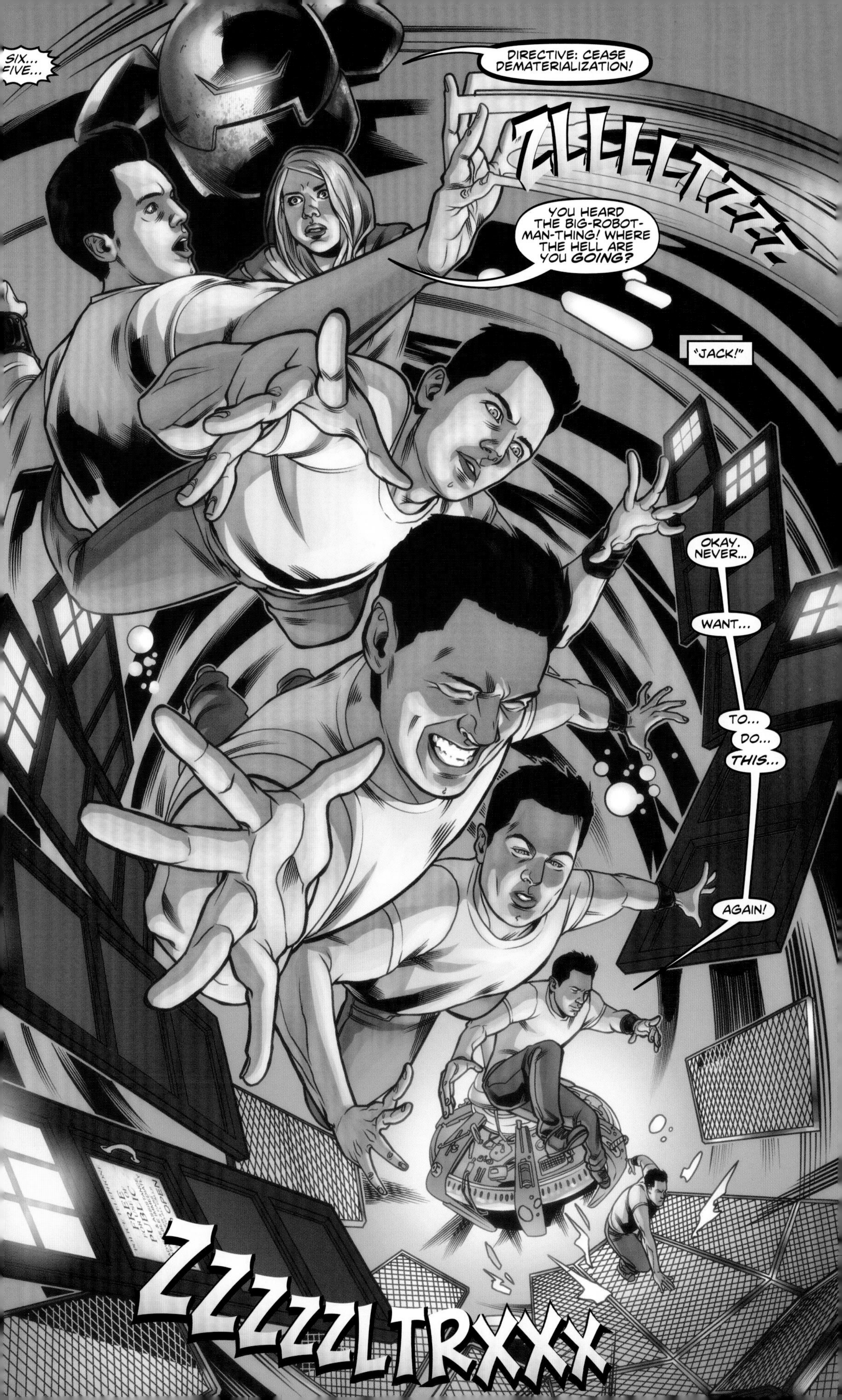
SIX... FIVE...
DIRECTIVE: CEASE DEMATERIALIZATION!
ZLLLLTZZZ
YOU HEARD THE BIG-ROBOT-MAN-THING! WHERE THE HELL ARE YOU GOING?
"JACK!"
OKAY. NEVER...
WANT...
TO...
DO...
THIS...
AGAIN!
ZZZZZLTRXXX

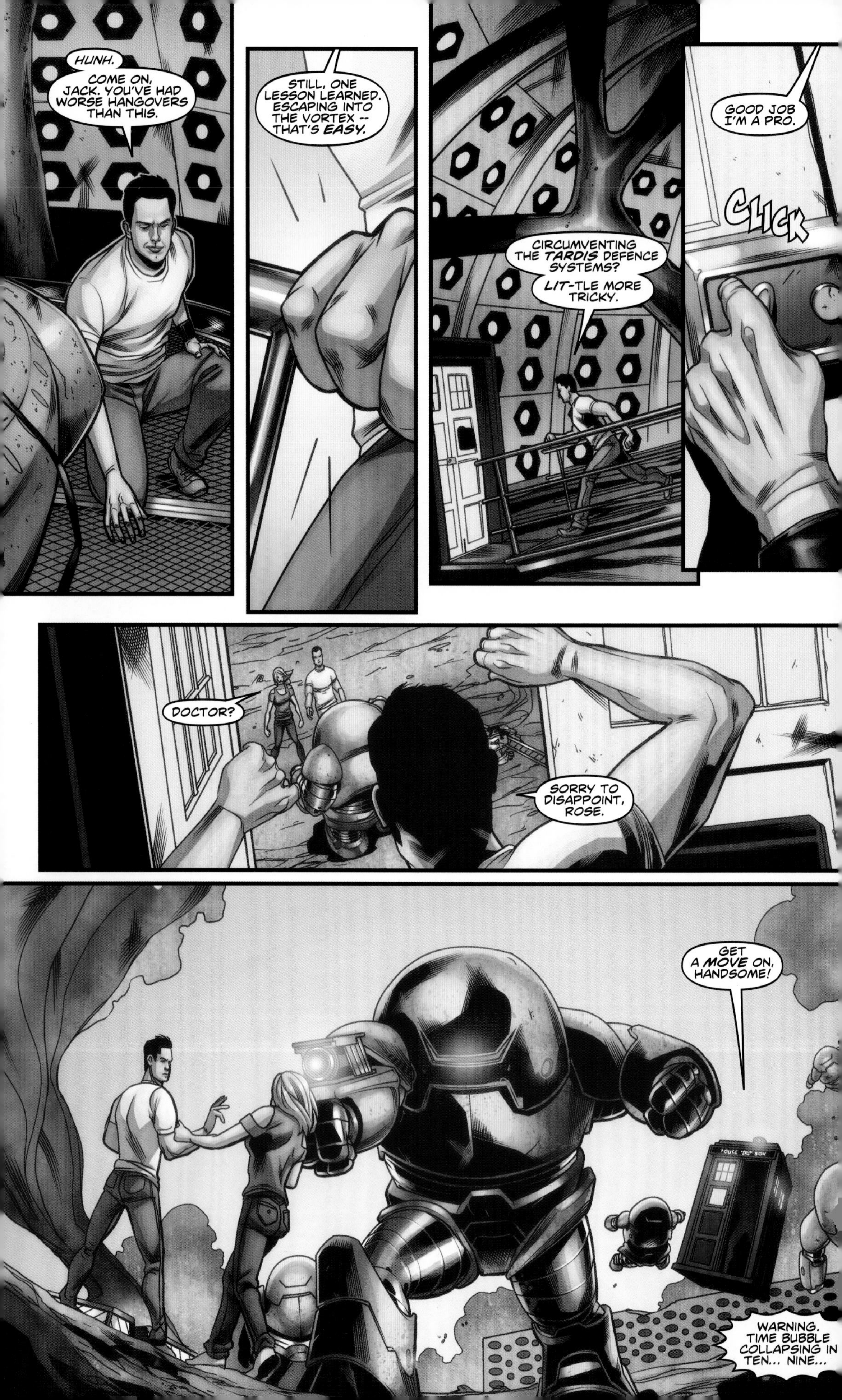
HUNH.
COME ON, JACK. YOU'VE HAD WORSE HANGOVERS THAN THIS.
STILL, ONE LESSON LEARNED. ESCAPING INTO THE VORTEX -- THAT'S EASY.
CIRCUMVENTING THE TARDIS DEFENCE SYSTEMS?
LIT-TLE MORE TRICKY.
GOOD JOB I'M A PRO.
CLICK
DOCTOR?
SORRY TO DISAPPOINT, ROSE.
GET A MOVE ON, HANDSOME!
WARNING. TIME BUBBLE COLLAPSING IN TEN... NINE...

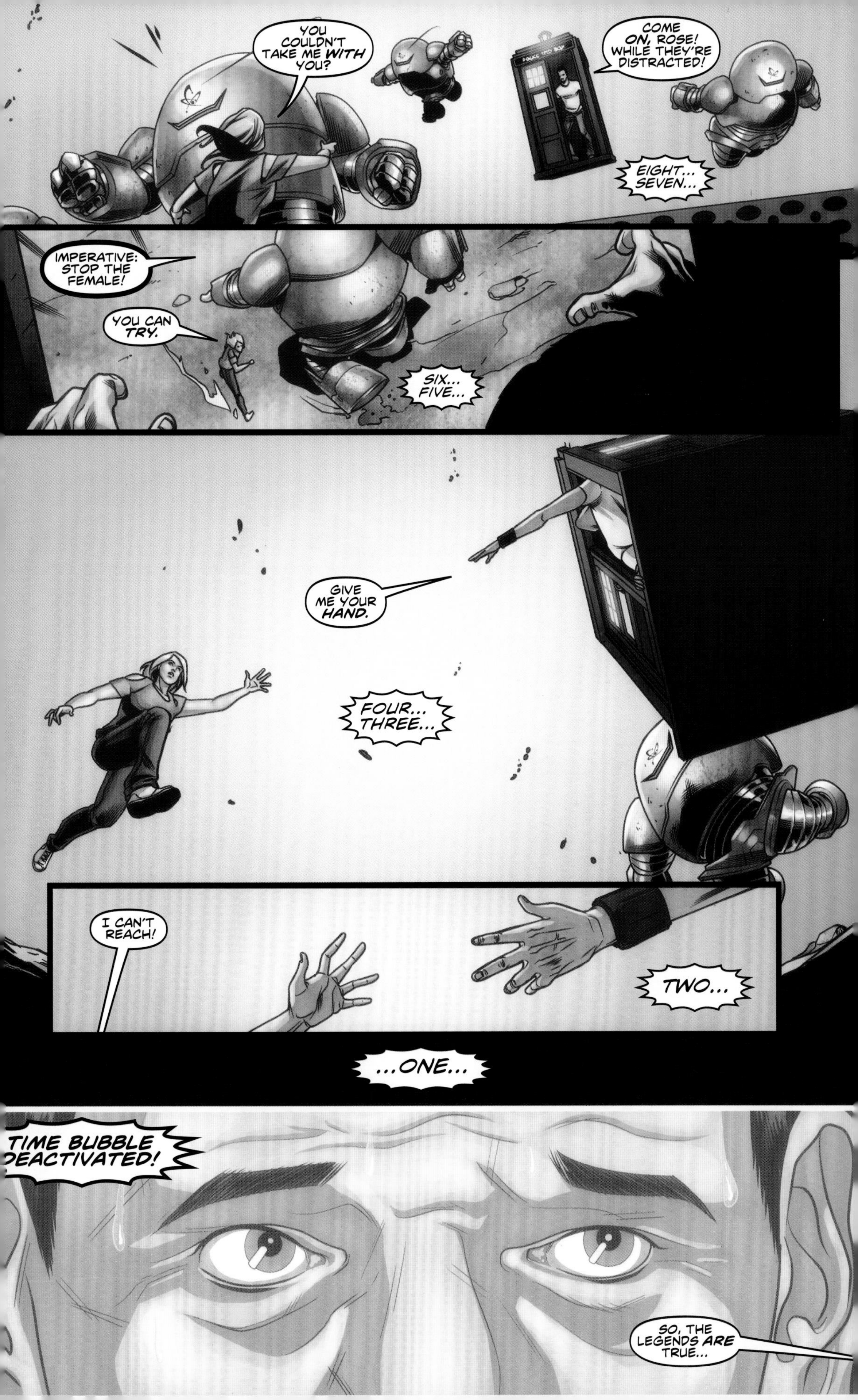
YOU COULDN'T TAKE ME WITH YOU?
COME ON, ROSE! WHILE THEY'RE DISTRACTED!
EIGHT... SEVEN...
IMPERATIVE: STOP THE FEMALE!
YOU CAN TRY.
SIX... FIVE...
GIVE ME YOUR HAND.
FOUR... THREE...
I CAN'T REACH!
TWO...
...ONE...
TIME BUBBLE DEACTIVATED!
SO, THE LEGENDS ARE TRUE...

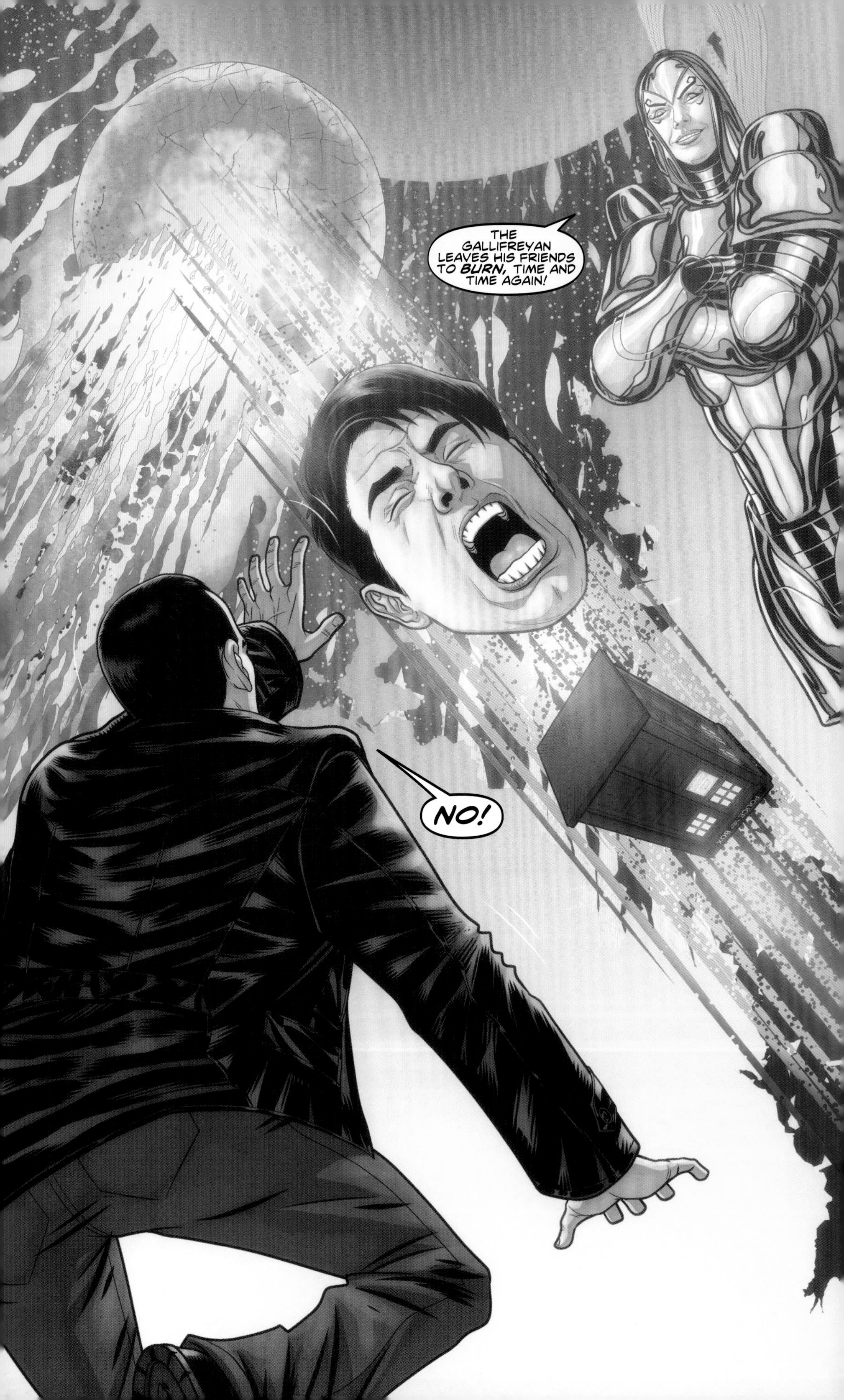
THE GALLIFREYAN LEAVES HIS FRIENDS TO BURN, TIME AND TIME AGAIN!
NO!

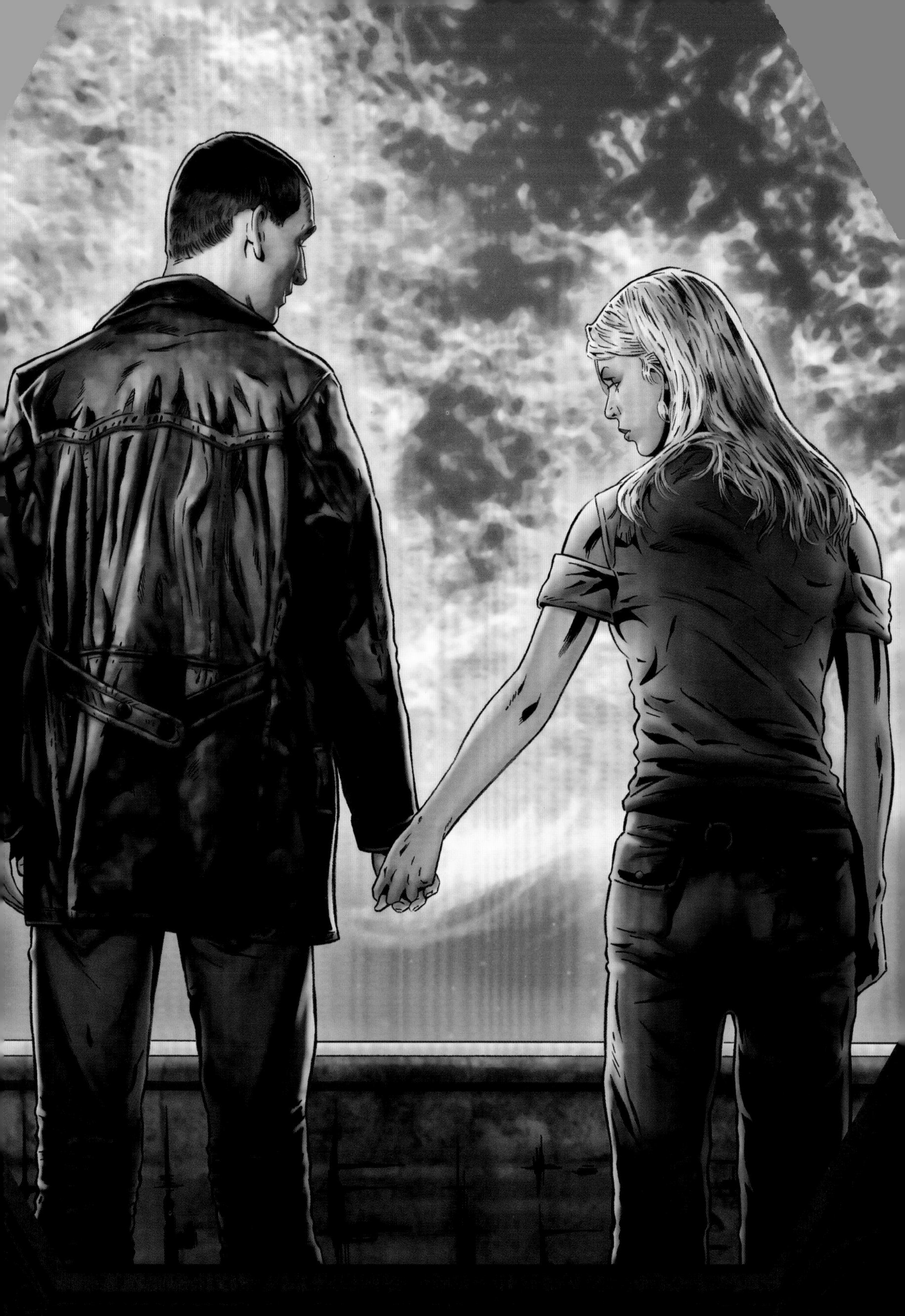

9D #1 Books A Million Cover: JOE CORRONEY

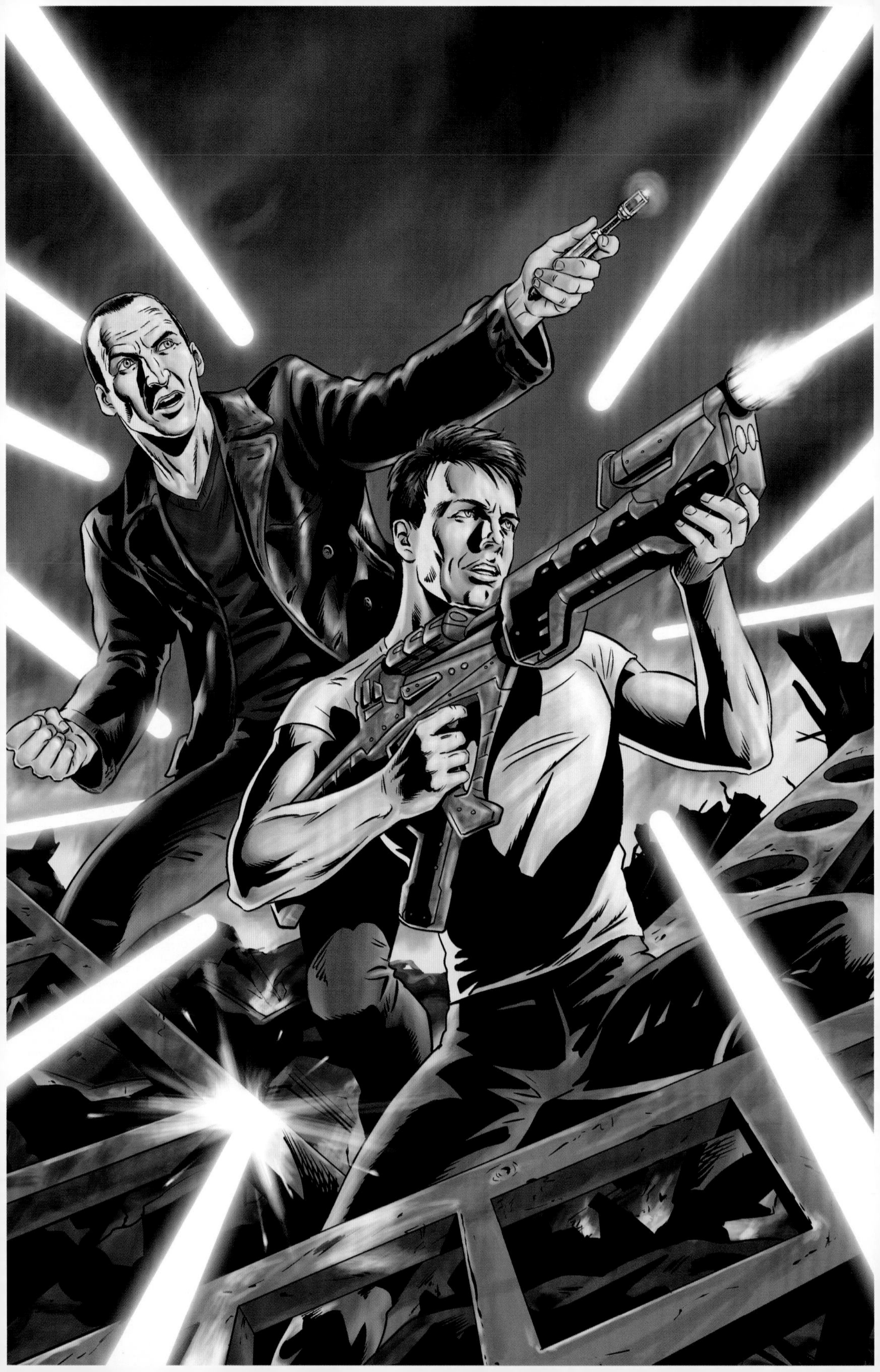

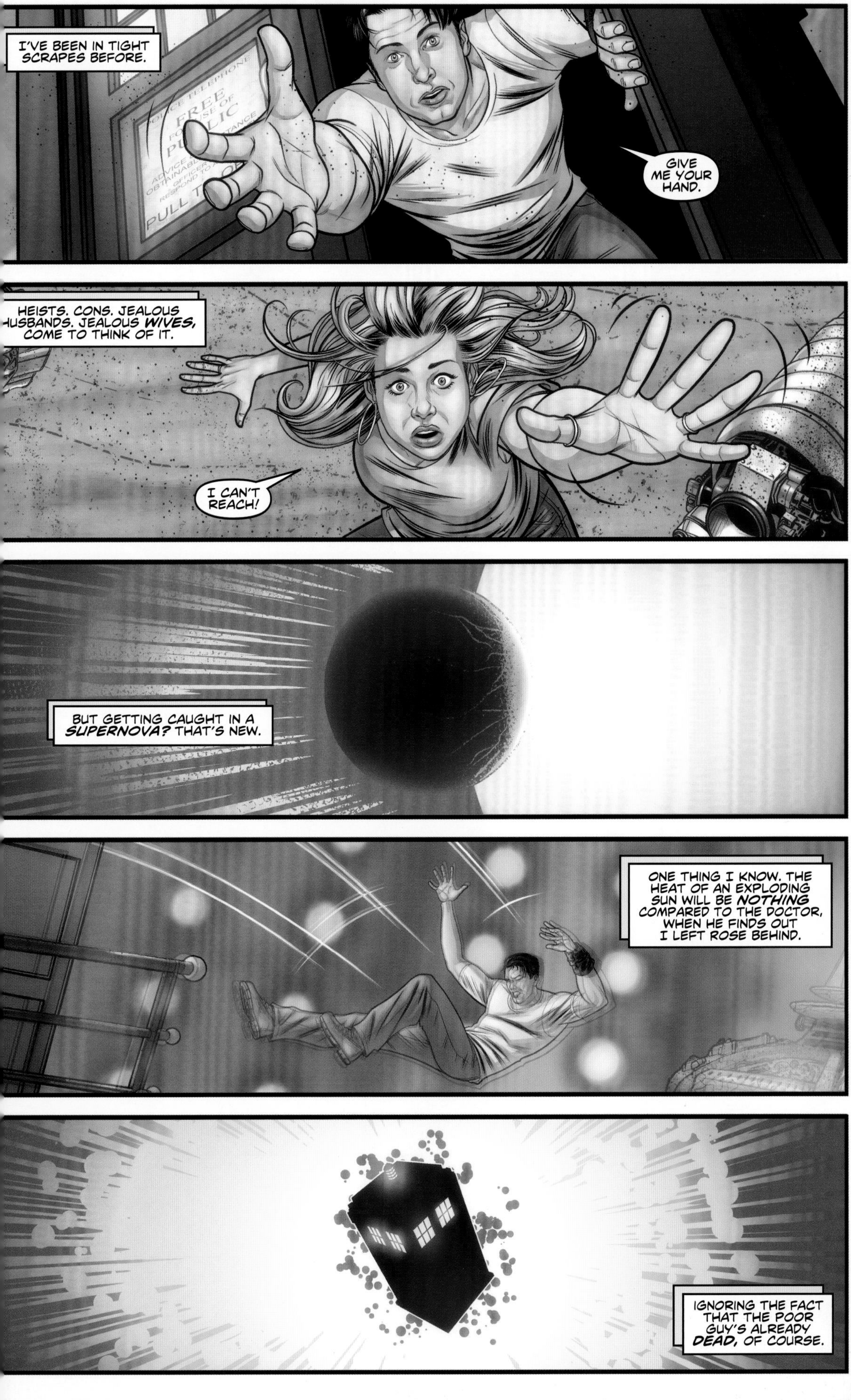

I'VE BEEN IN TIGHT SCRAPES BEFORE.
POLICE TELEPHONE FREE FOR USE OF PUBLIC ADVICE & ASSISTANCE OBTAINABLE IMMEDIATELY OFFICERS & CARS RESPOND TO ALL CALLS PULL TO OPEN
GIVE ME YOUR HAND.
HEISTS. CONS. JEALOUS HUSBANDS. JEALOUS WIVES, COME TO THINK OF IT.
I CAN'T REACH!
BUT GETTING CAUGHT IN A SUPERNOVA? THAT'S NEW.
ONE THING I KNOW. THE HEAT OF AN EXPLODING SUN WILL BE NOTHING COMPARED TO THE DOCTOR, WHEN HE FINDS OUT I LEFT ROSE BEHIND.
IGNORING THE FACT THAT THE POOR GUY'S ALREADY DEAD, OF COURSE.

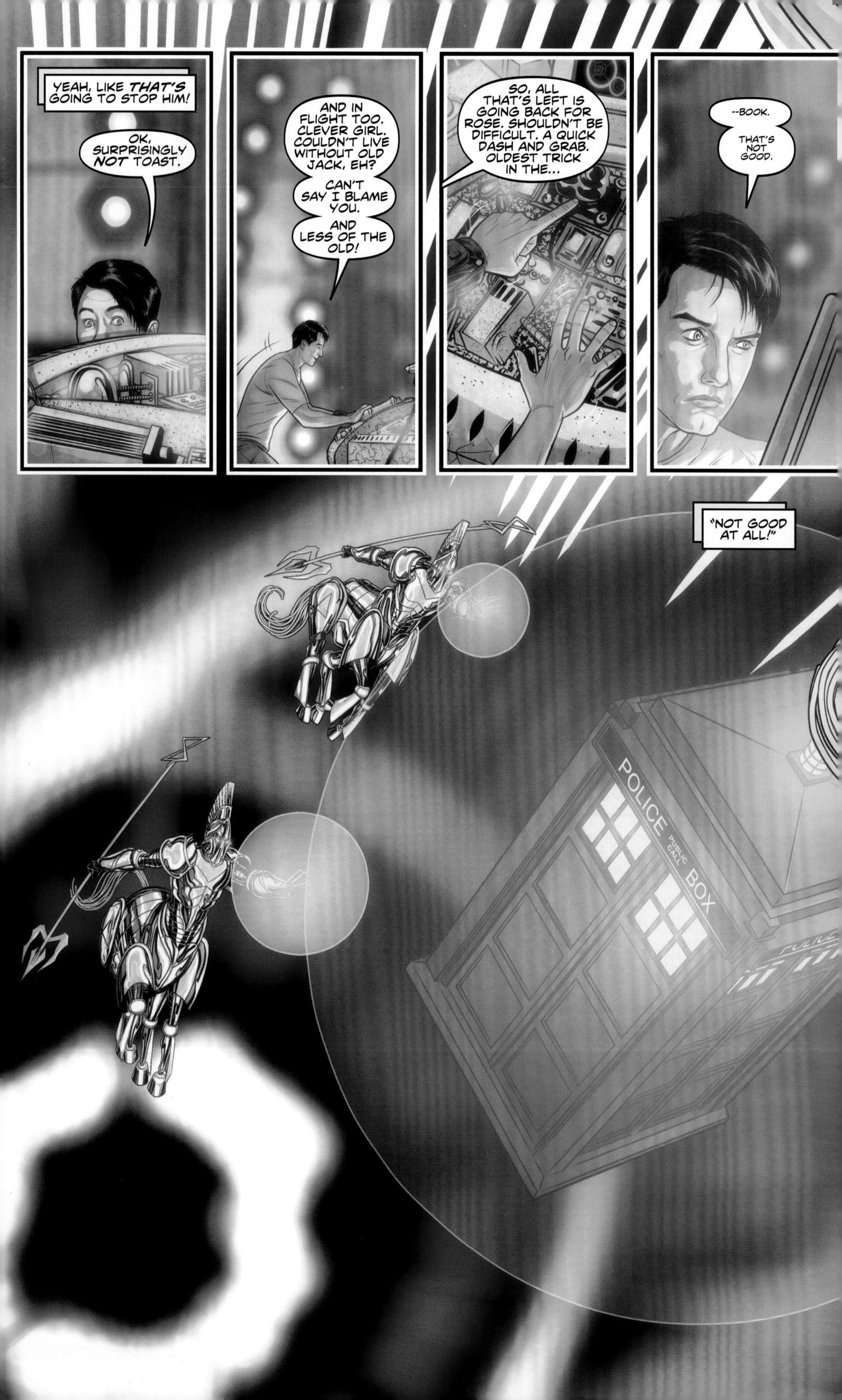
YEAH, LIKE THAT'S GOING TO STOP HIM!
OK, SURPRISINGLY NOT TOAST.
AND IN FLIGHT TOO. CLEVER GIRL. COULDN'T LIVE WITHOUT OLD JACK, EH?
CAN'T SAY I BLAME YOU.
AND LESS OF THE OLD!
SO, ALL THAT'S LEFT IS GOING BACK FOR ROSE. SHOULDN'T BE DIFFICULT. A QUICK DASH AND GRAB. OLDEST TRICK IN THE...
--BOOK.
THAT'S NOT GOOD.
"NOT GOOD AT ALL!"
POLICE PUBLIC CALL BOX

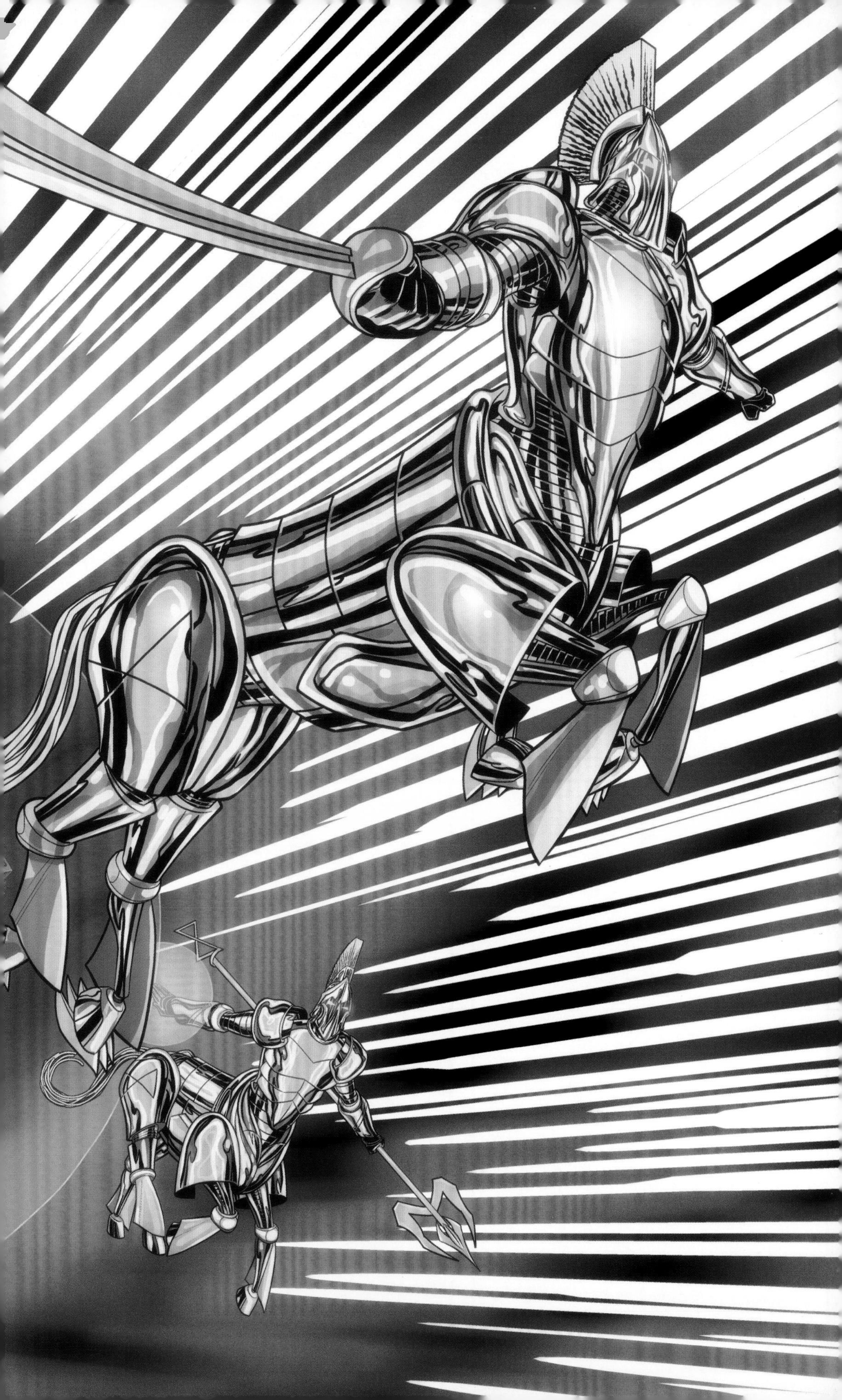

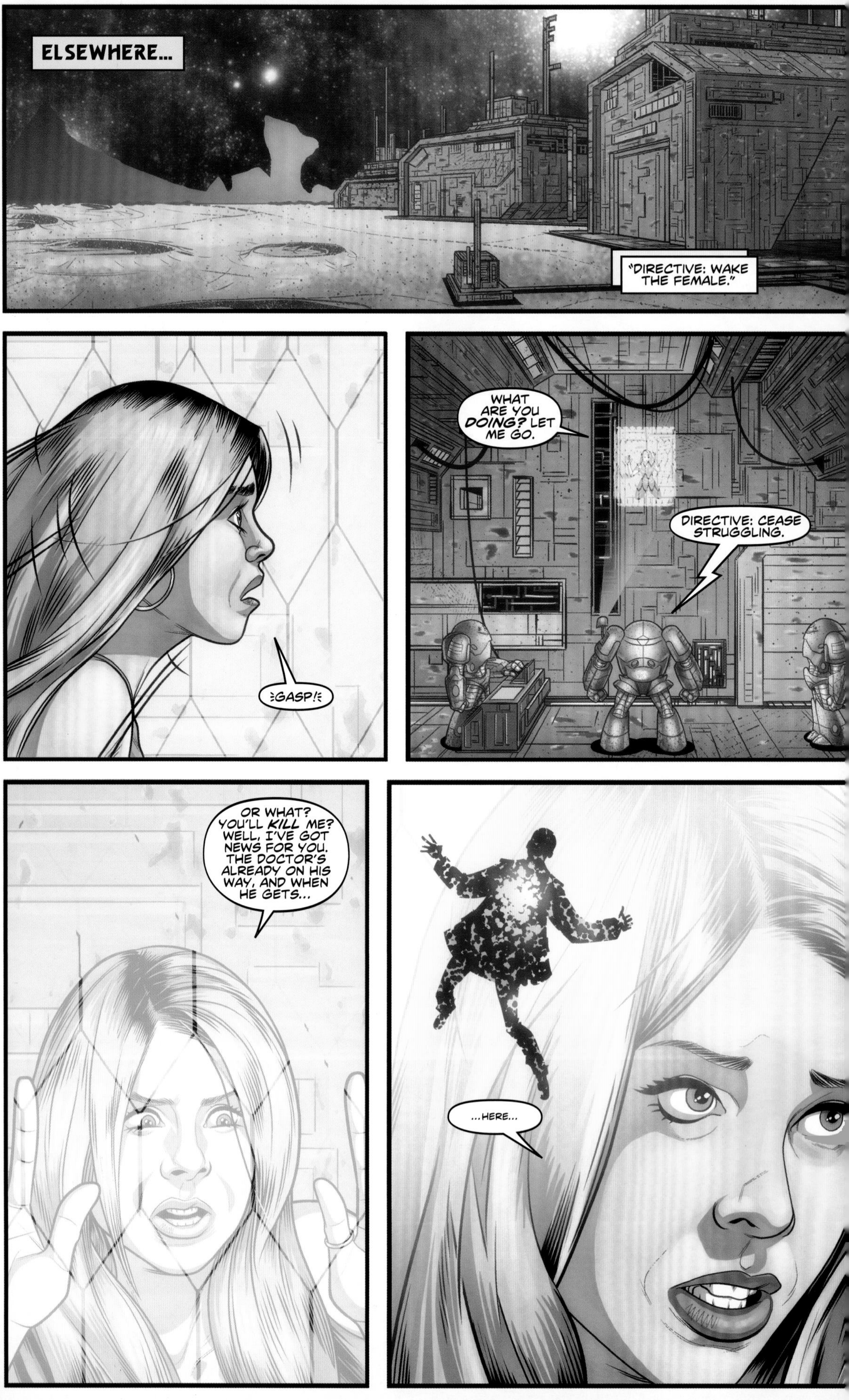

ELSEWHERE...
"DIRECTIVE: WAKE THE FEMALE."
:GASP!:
WHAT ARE YOU DOING? LET ME GO.
DIRECTIVE: CEASE STRUGGLING.
OR WHAT? YOU'LL KILL ME? WELL, I'VE GOT NEWS FOR YOU. THE DOCTOR'S ALREADY ON HIS WAY, AND WHEN HE GETS...
...HERE...

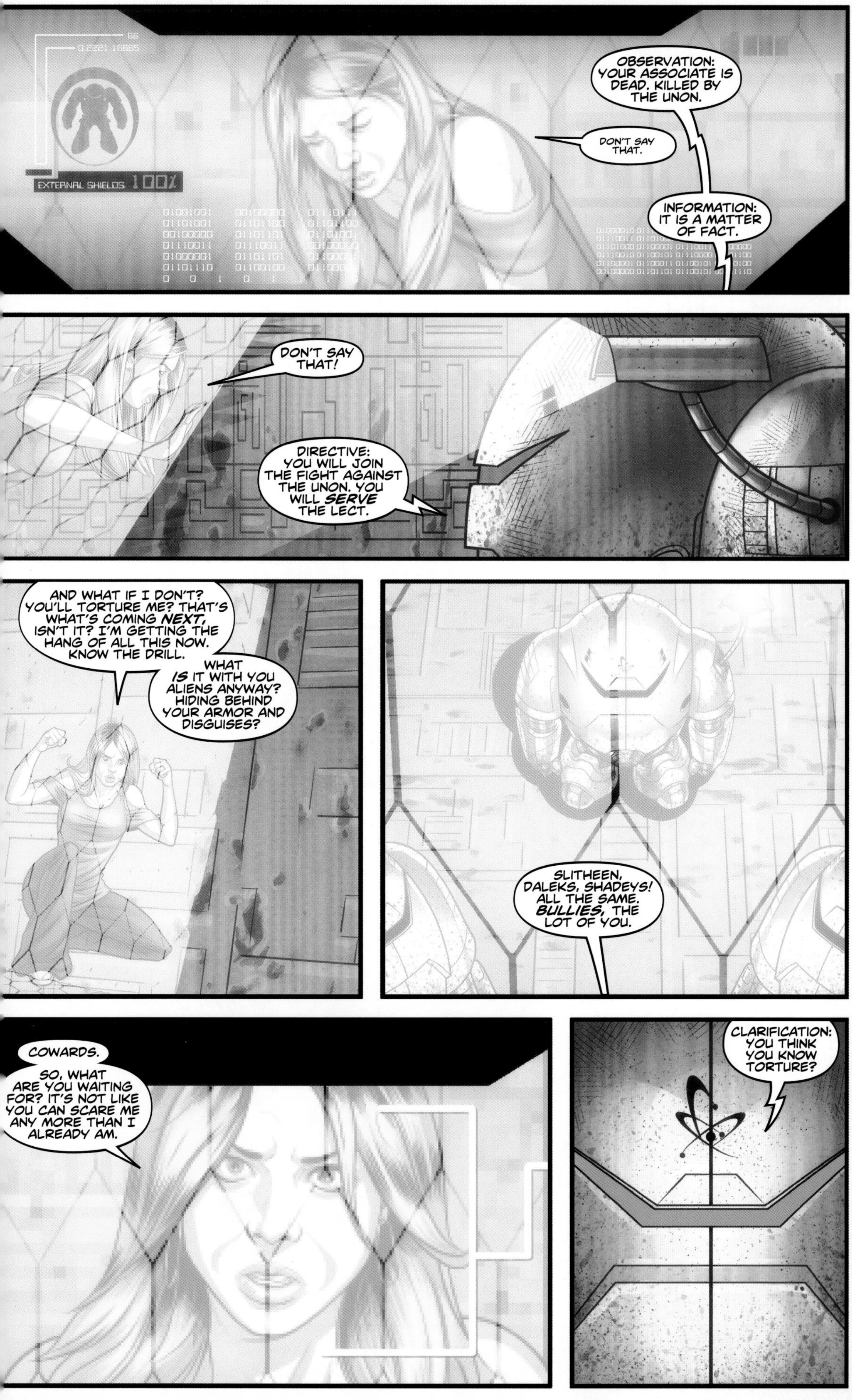
EXTERNAL SHIELDS: 100%
OBSERVATION: YOUR ASSOCIATE IS DEAD. KILLED BY THE UNON.
DON'T SAY THAT.
INFORMATION: IT IS A MATTER OF FACT.
DON'T SAY THAT!
DIRECTIVE: YOU WILL JOIN THE FIGHT AGAINST THE UNON. YOU WILL SERVE THE LECT.
AND WHAT IF I DON'T? YOU'LL TORTURE ME? THAT'S WHAT'S COMING NEXT, ISN'T IT? I'M GETTING THE HANG OF ALL THIS NOW. KNOW THE DRILL.
WHAT IS IT WITH YOU ALIENS ANYWAY? HIDING BEHIND YOUR ARMOR AND DISGUISES?
SLITHEEN, DALEKS, SHADEYS! ALL THE SAME. BULLIES, THE LOT OF YOU.
COWARDS.
SO, WHAT ARE YOU WAITING FOR? IT'S NOT LIKE YOU CAN SCARE ME ANY MORE THAN I ALREADY AM.
CLARIFICATION: YOU THINK YOU KNOW TORTURE?

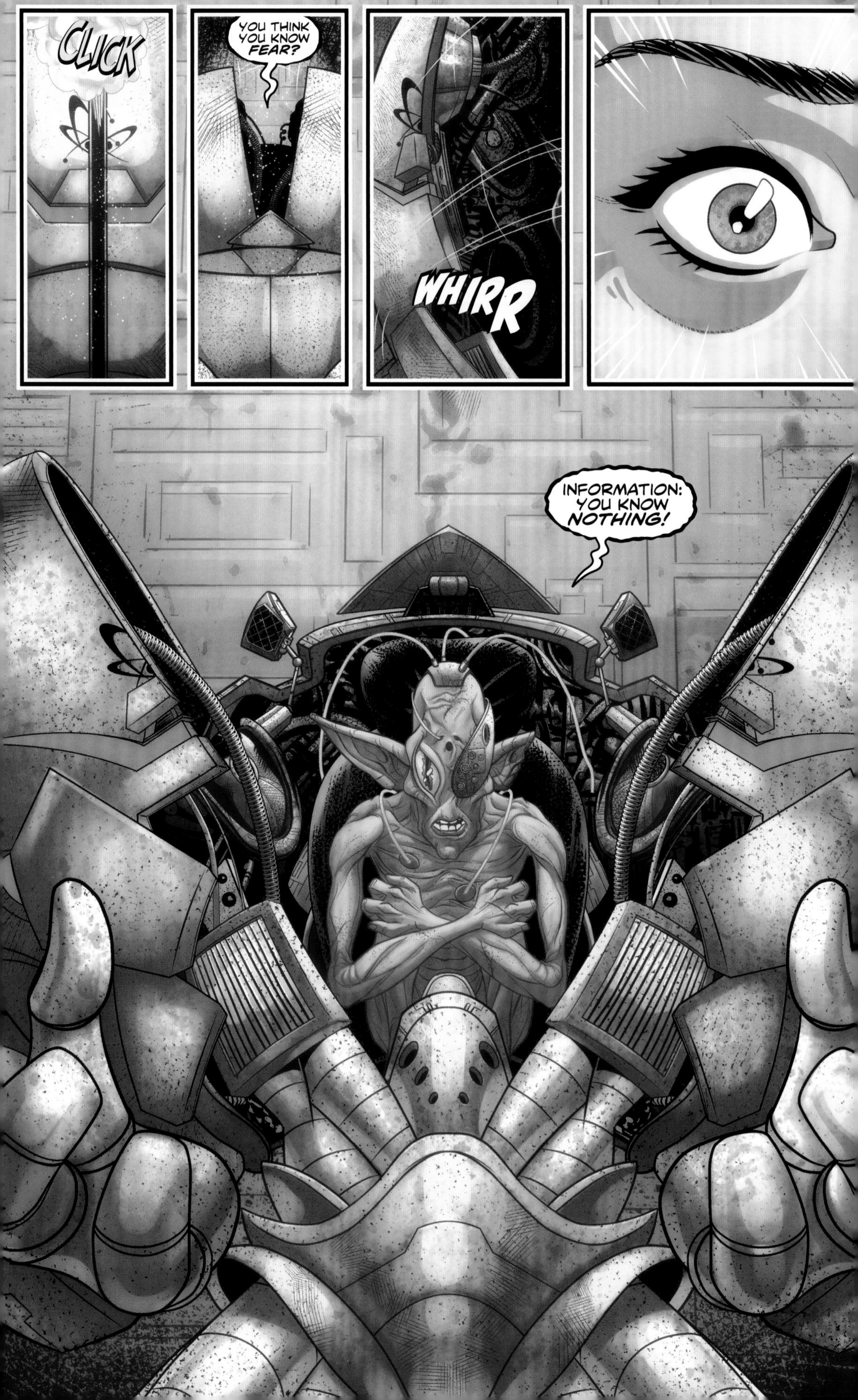
CLICK
YOU THINK YOU KNOW FEAR?
WHIRR
INFORMATION: YOU KNOW NOTHING!

LOOK, CAN'T WE COME TO SOME KIND OF ARRANGEMENT?

YOU SHOW ME WHAT CONTROLS WILL HELP US ESCAPE OUR FOUR-LEGGED FRIENDS, AND I DON'T TAKE A COMPACT LASER DELUXE TO YOUR CENTRAL COLUMN.

WOAH, THERE! I WAS ONLY JOKING.

ANYONE EVER TOLD YOU, YOU'RE KINDA TOUCHY FOR A TIME MACHINE.

BUT IF WE'RE MAKING IT PERSONAL, HOW ABOUT I HAMMER MY POINT HOME? EITHER YOU MAKE AN EMERGENCY LANDING OR--

JACK!

DOCTOR, YOU'RE--

ALIVE, YEAH, WHICH IS MORE THAN WILL BE SAID FOR YOU IF I FIND A SINGLE SCRATCH ON THAT CONSOLE!

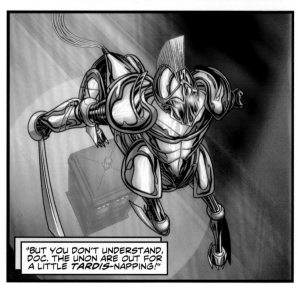

"BUT YOU DON'T UNDERSTAND, DOC. THE UNON ARE OUT FOR A LITTLE TARDIS-NAPPING!"

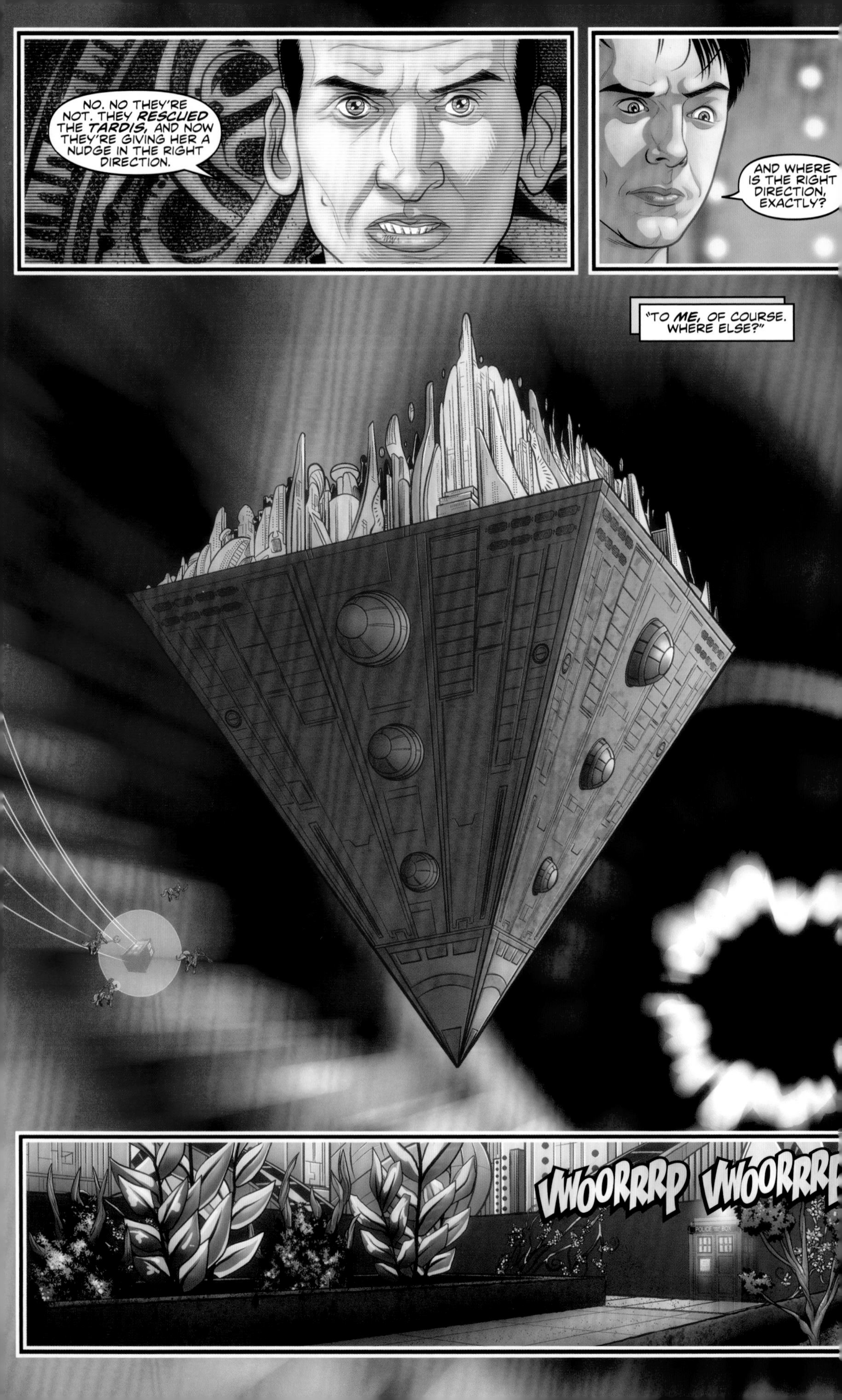
NO. NO THEY'RE NOT. THEY RESCUED THE TARDIS, AND NOW THEY'RE GIVING HER A NUDGE IN THE RIGHT DIRECTION.
AND WHERE IS THE RIGHT DIRECTION, EXACTLY?
"TO ME, OF COURSE. WHERE ELSE?"
VWOORRRP VWOORRRP
POLICE BOX

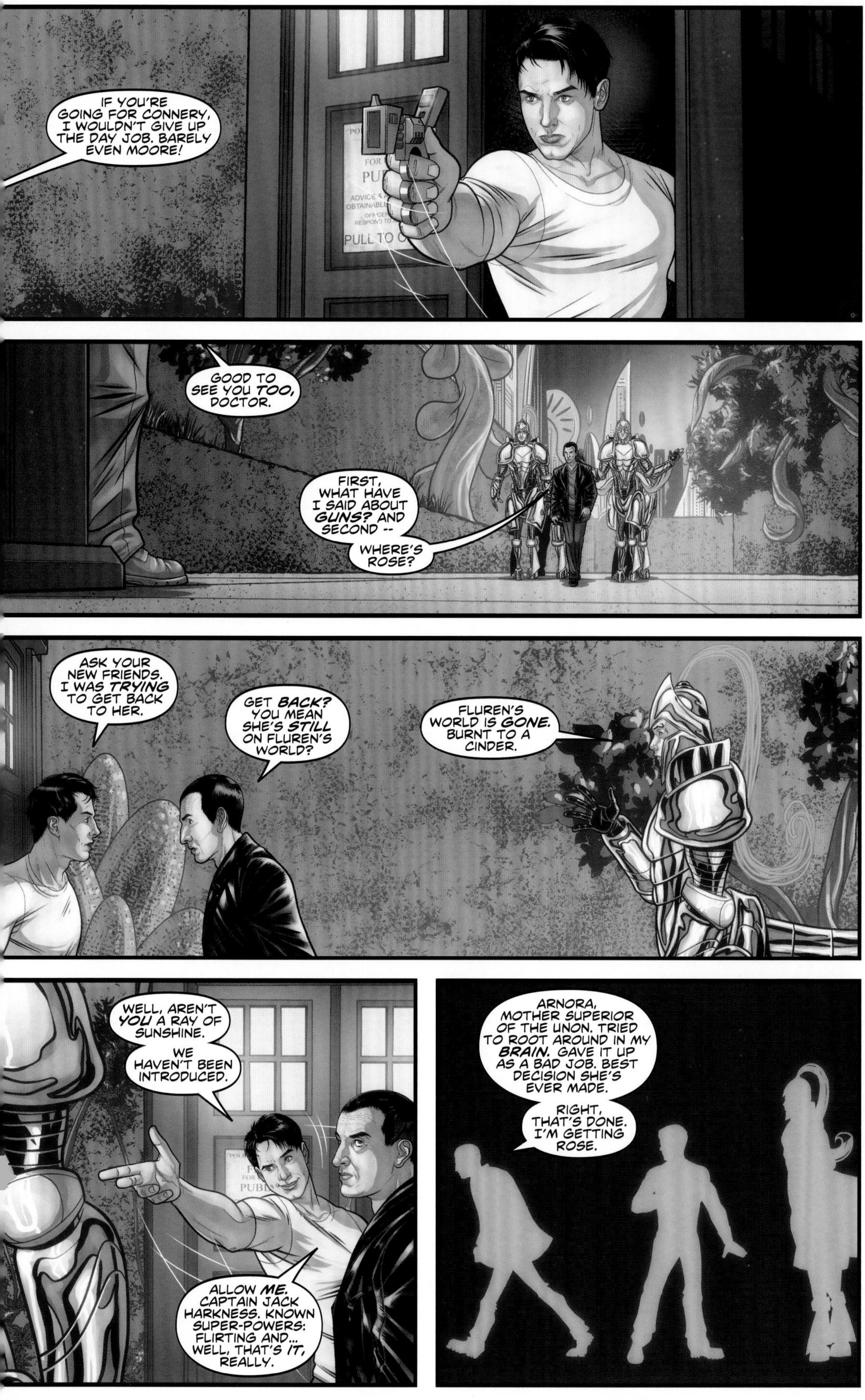
IF YOU'RE GOING FOR CONNERY, I WOULDN'T GIVE UP THE DAY JOB. BARELY EVEN MOORE!
POLICE
FOR
PUB
ADVICE &
OBTAINABLE
OFFICER
RESPOND TO
PULL TO O
GOOD TO SEE YOU TOO, DOCTOR.
FIRST, WHAT HAVE I SAID ABOUT GUNS? AND SECOND --
WHERE'S ROSE?
ASK YOUR NEW FRIENDS. I WAS TRYING TO GET BACK TO HER.
GET BACK? YOU MEAN SHE'S STILL ON FLUREN'S WORLD?
FLUREN'S WORLD IS GONE. BURNT TO A CINDER.
WELL, AREN'T YOU A RAY OF SUNSHINE.
WE HAVEN'T BEEN INTRODUCED.
ALLOW ME. CAPTAIN JACK HARKNESS. KNOWN SUPER-POWERS: FLIRTING AND... WELL, THAT'S IT, REALLY.
ARNORA, MOTHER SUPERIOR OF THE UNON. TRIED TO ROOT AROUND IN MY BRAIN. GAVE IT UP AS A BAD JOB. BEST DECISION SHE'S EVER MADE.
RIGHT, THAT'S DONE. I'M GETTING ROSE.

THE HUMAN IS NOT ON FLUREN'S WORLD.

SORRY, AND YOU ARE?

EVJA -- GRAND HIGH SEER OF THE UNON, OBSERVER OF THE SEVEN REALITIES, DEFENDER OF THE--

YEAH, YEAH, VERY IMPRESSIVE. USED TO HAVE LOADS OF TITLES MYSELF. NOW JUST STICK TO THE ONE. YOU WERE SAYING SOMETHING ABOUT A *HUMAN?*

SHE IS IN A *FORBIDDEN* SECTOR OF TIME.

NO SUCH THING WHERE I'M CONCERNED. COME ON JACK, WE'RE LEAVING.

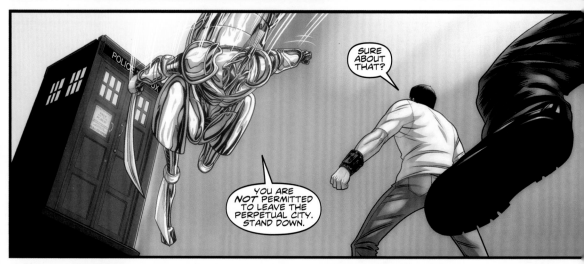

SURE ABOUT THAT?

YOU ARE *NOT* PERMITTED TO LEAVE THE PERPETUAL CITY. STAND DOWN.

STAND DOWN?

YOU DON'T WANT TO DO THIS. NOT TO *ME.* UP TO NOW, I'VE BEEN PATIENT. UP TO NOW, I'VE BEEN *NICE.* GET OUT OF MY WAY OR YOU'LL DISCOVER WHAT I'M LIKE THE *REST* OF THE TIME.

YOU MUST CALM YOURSELF, DOCTOR.

MUST I? YOU APOLOGIZED FOR THE MIND PROBE AND I APPRECIATE THAT. I EVEN SAID I'D *CO-OPERATE,* BUT NOT WHEN ROSE IS IN DANGER. THAT'S A DEAL-BREAKER, RIGHT THERE.

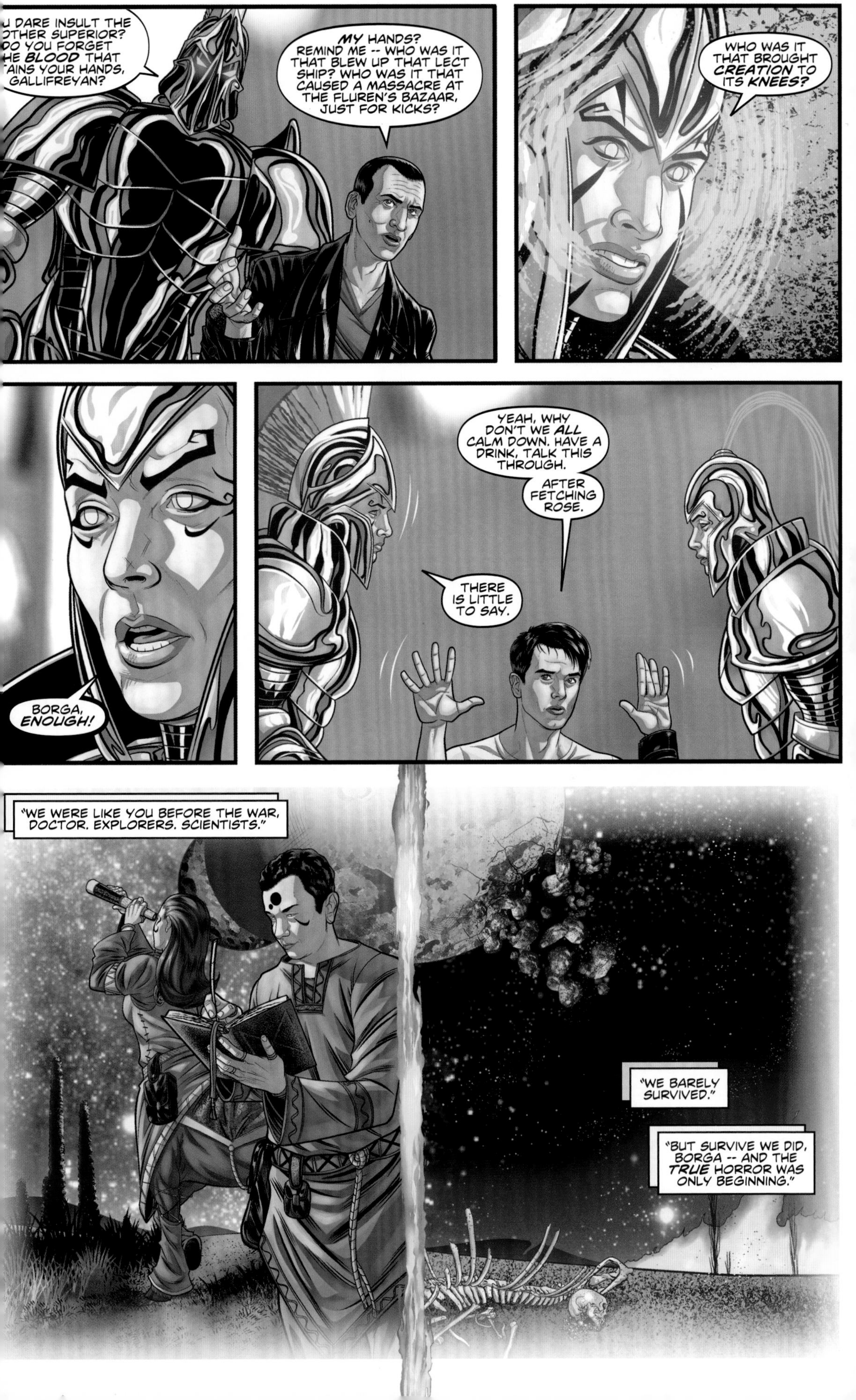
U DARE INSULT THE OTHER SUPERIOR? DO YOU FORGET HE BLOOD THAT TAINS YOUR HANDS, GALLIFREYAN?
MY HANDS? REMIND ME -- WHO WAS IT THAT BLEW UP THAT LECT SHIP? WHO WAS IT THAT CAUSED A MASSACRE AT THE FLUREN'S BAZAAR, JUST FOR KICKS?
WHO WAS IT THAT BROUGHT CREATION TO ITS KNEES?
BORGA, ENOUGH!
YEAH, WHY DON'T WE ALL CALM DOWN. HAVE A DRINK, TALK THIS THROUGH.
AFTER FETCHING ROSE.
THERE IS LITTLE TO SAY.
"WE WERE LIKE YOU BEFORE THE WAR, DOCTOR. EXPLORERS. SCIENTISTS."
"WE BARELY SURVIVED."
"BUT SURVIVE WE DID, BORGA -- AND THE TRUE HORROR WAS ONLY BEGINNING."

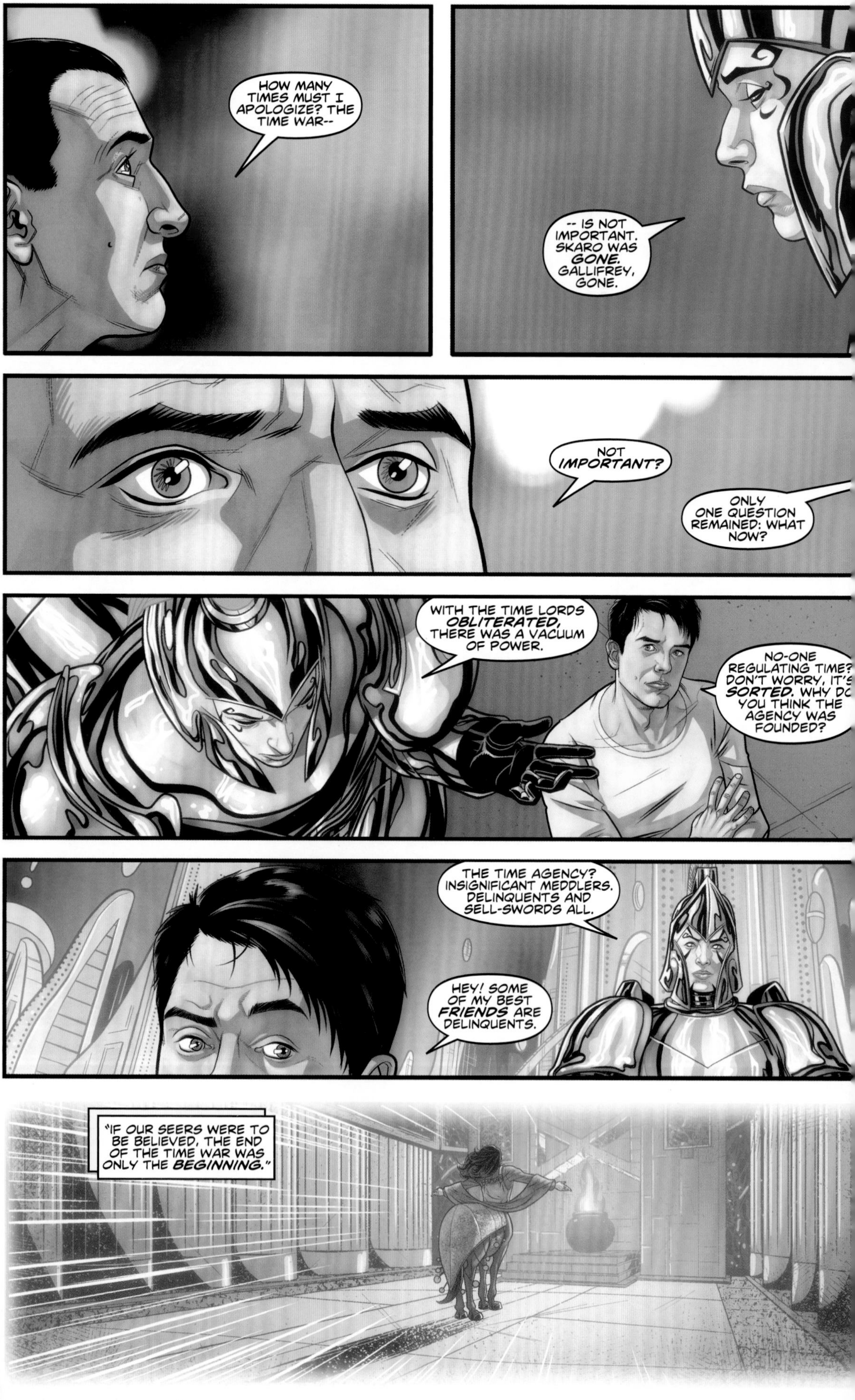
HOW MANY TIMES MUST I APOLOGIZE? THE TIME WAR--
-- IS NOT IMPORTANT. SKARO WAS GONE. GALLIFREY, GONE.
NOT IMPORTANT?
ONLY ONE QUESTION REMAINED: WHAT NOW?
WITH THE TIME LORDS OBLITERATED, THERE WAS A VACUUM OF POWER.
NO-ONE REGULATING TIME? DON'T WORRY, IT'S SORTED. WHY DO YOU THINK THE AGENCY WAS FOUNDED?
THE TIME AGENCY? INSIGNIFICANT MEDDLERS. DELINQUENTS AND SELL-SWORDS ALL.
HEY! SOME OF MY BEST FRIENDS ARE DELINQUENTS.
"IF OUR SEERS WERE TO BE BELIEVED, THE END OF THE TIME WAR WAS ONLY THE BEGINNING."

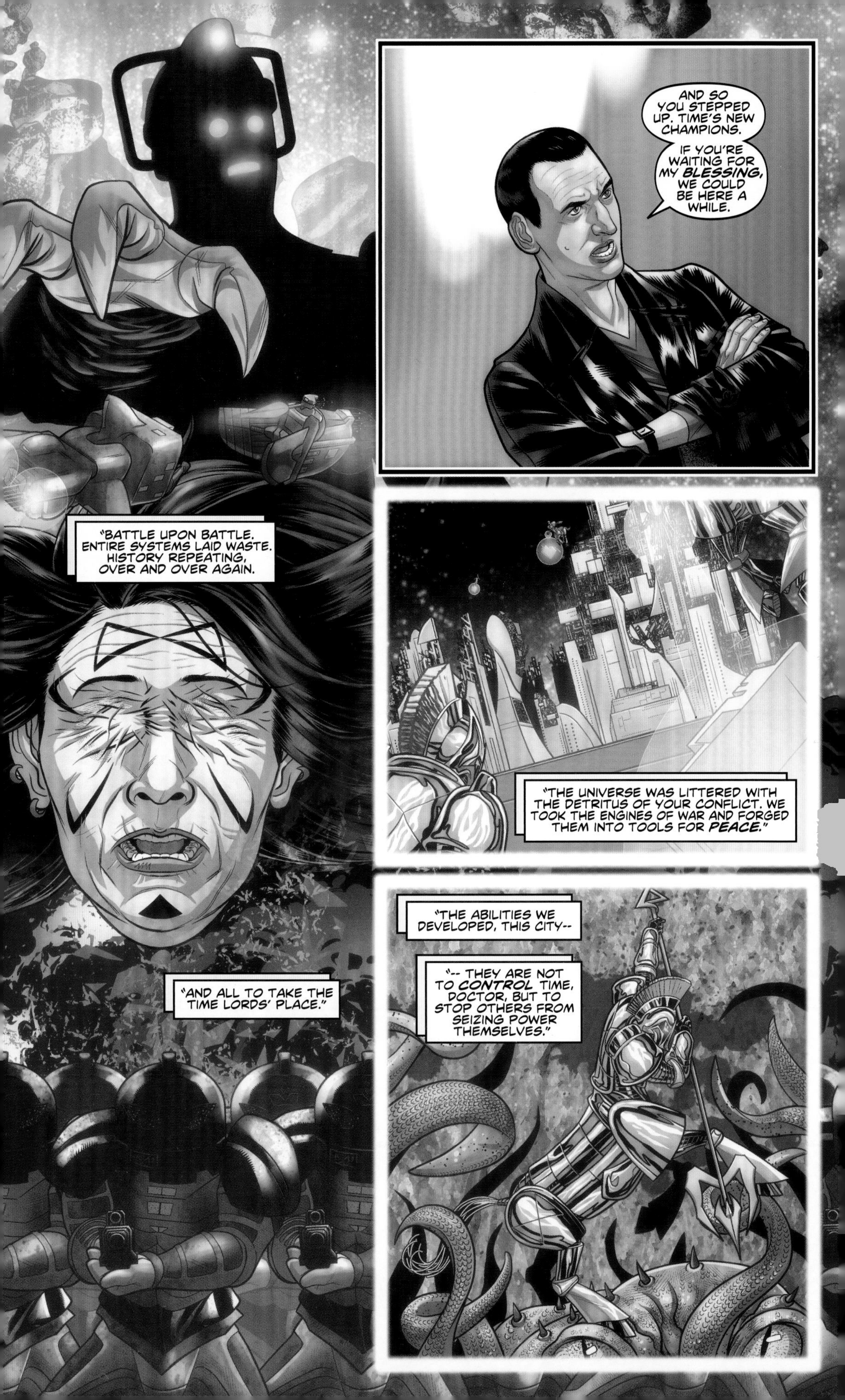
AND SO YOU STEPPED UP. TIME'S NEW CHAMPIONS.
IF YOU'RE WAITING FOR MY *BLESSING*, WE COULD BE HERE A WHILE.
"BATTLE UPON BATTLE. ENTIRE SYSTEMS LAID WASTE. HISTORY REPEATING, OVER AND OVER AGAIN.
"THE UNIVERSE WAS LITTERED WITH THE DETRITUS OF YOUR CONFLICT. WE TOOK THE ENGINES OF WAR AND FORGED THEM INTO TOOLS FOR *PEACE*."
"AND ALL TO TAKE THE TIME LORDS' PLACE."
"THE ABILITIES WE DEVELOPED, THIS CITY--
"-- THEY ARE NOT TO *CONTROL* TIME, DOCTOR, BUT TO STOP OTHERS FROM SEIZING POWER THEMSELVES."

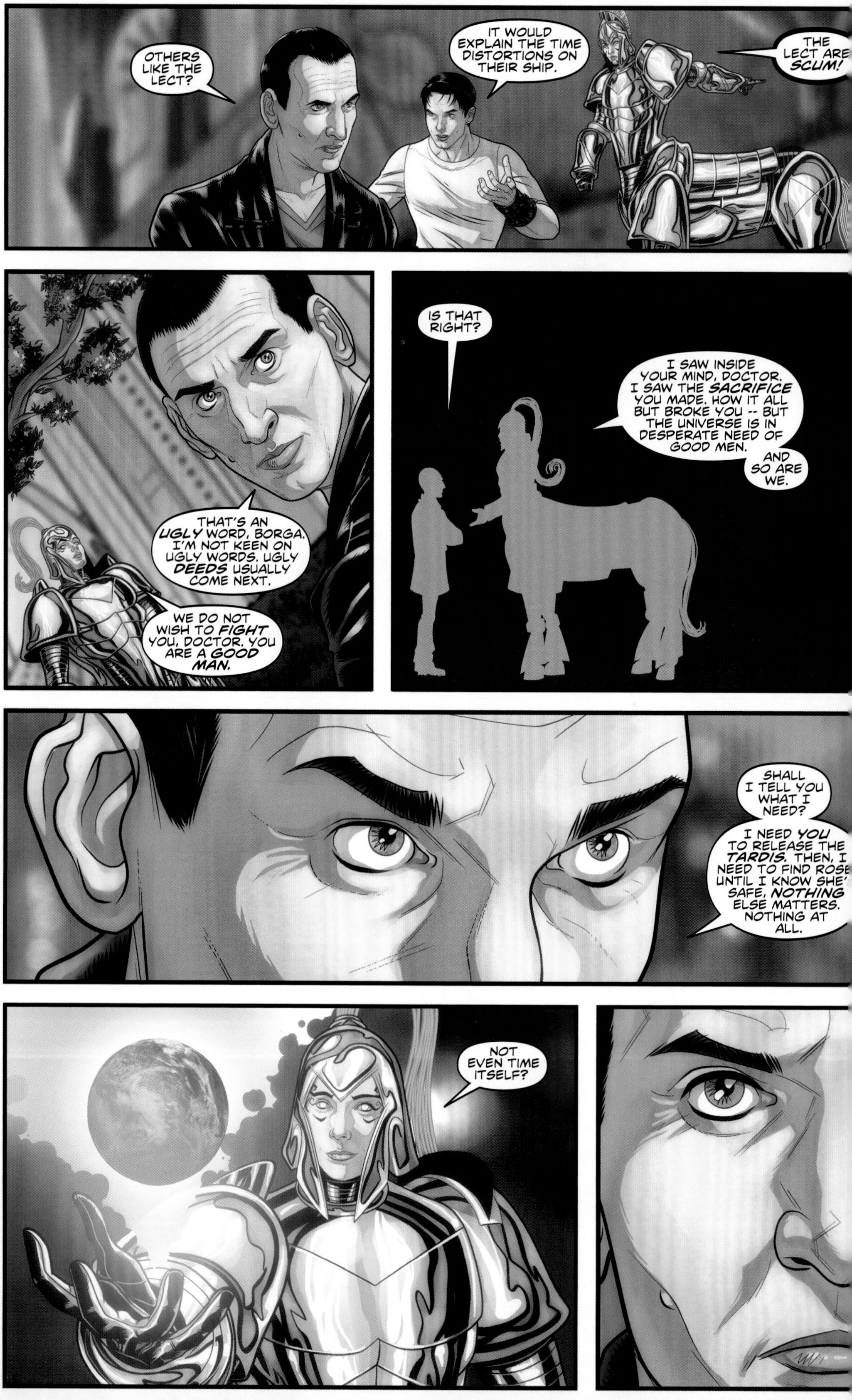
OTHERS LIKE THE LECT?
IT WOULD EXPLAIN THE TIME DISTORTIONS ON THEIR SHIP.
THE LECT ARE SCUM!
THAT'S AN UGLY WORD, BORGA. I'M NOT KEEN ON UGLY WORDS. UGLY DEEDS USUALLY COME NEXT.
WE DO NOT WISH TO FIGHT YOU, DOCTOR. YOU ARE A GOOD MAN.
IS THAT RIGHT?
I SAW INSIDE YOUR MIND, DOCTOR. I SAW THE SACRIFICE YOU MADE. HOW IT ALL BUT BROKE YOU -- BUT THE UNIVERSE IS IN DESPERATE NEED OF GOOD MEN.
AND SO ARE WE.
SHALL I TELL YOU WHAT I NEED?
I NEED YOU TO RELEASE THE TARDIS. THEN, I NEED TO FIND ROSE. UNTIL I KNOW SHE'S SAFE, NOTHING ELSE MATTERS. NOTHING AT ALL.
NOT EVEN TIME ITSELF?

... WHAT IS THIS?

A FRACTURE IN TIME. THE TIME WAR HAS LEFT *FISSURES* RUNNING THROUGH THE VERY FABRIC OF THE UNIVERSE. CHRONAL FAULT LINES.

THE PLANET IS *TRAXIS*, A CLASS-9 WORLD WITH A POPULATION OF 7.2 BILLION.

AND IT IS BEING TORN *APART*. A FAULT LINE HAS OPENED, THE PAST, PRESENT AND THE FUTURE CRASHING TOGETHER.

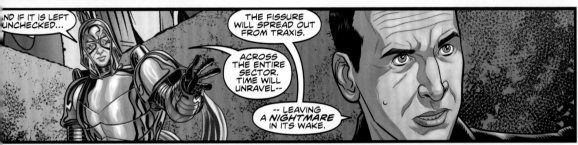

AND IF IT IS LEFT UNCHECKED...

THE FISSURE WILL SPREAD OUT FROM TRAXIS.

ACROSS THE ENTIRE SECTOR. TIME WILL UNRAVEL--

-- LEAVING A *NIGHTMARE* IN ITS WAKE.

A TEMPORAL STORM THAT WILL RAGE FOR MILLENNIA, MAYBE UNTIL THE END OF DAYS.

FORTUNATELY, WE HAVE A SOLUTION.

VZZZT

HANG ON --

"-- THAT'S A TEMPORAL STABILIZER."

"IT IS. IF ACTIVATED AT THE DISTORTION'S *EPICENTER*, IT WILL ACT AS A SUTURE, STITCHING TIME BACK TOGETHER."

"A *GALLIFREYAN* STABLIZER."

THEN WHO BETTER THAN A TIME LORD TO OPERATE IT?

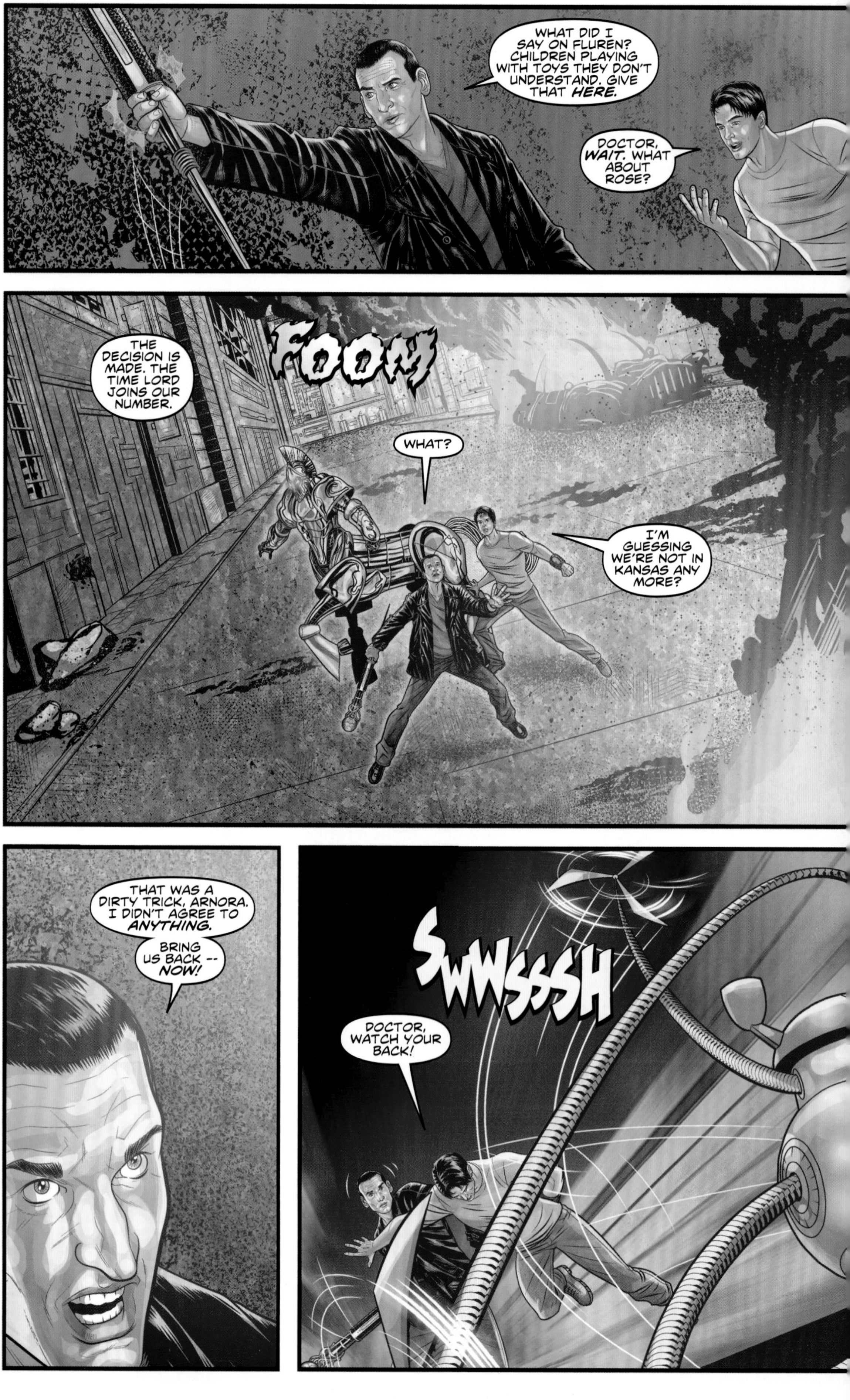
WHAT DID I SAY ON FLUREN? CHILDREN PLAYING WITH TOYS THEY DON'T UNDERSTAND. GIVE THAT HERE.
DOCTOR, WAIT. WHAT ABOUT ROSE?
THE DECISION IS MADE. THE TIME LORD JOINS OUR NUMBER.
FOOM
WHAT?
I'M GUESSING WE'RE NOT IN KANSAS ANY MORE?
THAT WAS A DIRTY TRICK, ARNORA. I DIDN'T AGREE TO ANYTHING.
BRING US BACK -- NOW!
SWWSSSH
DOCTOR, WATCH YOUR BACK!

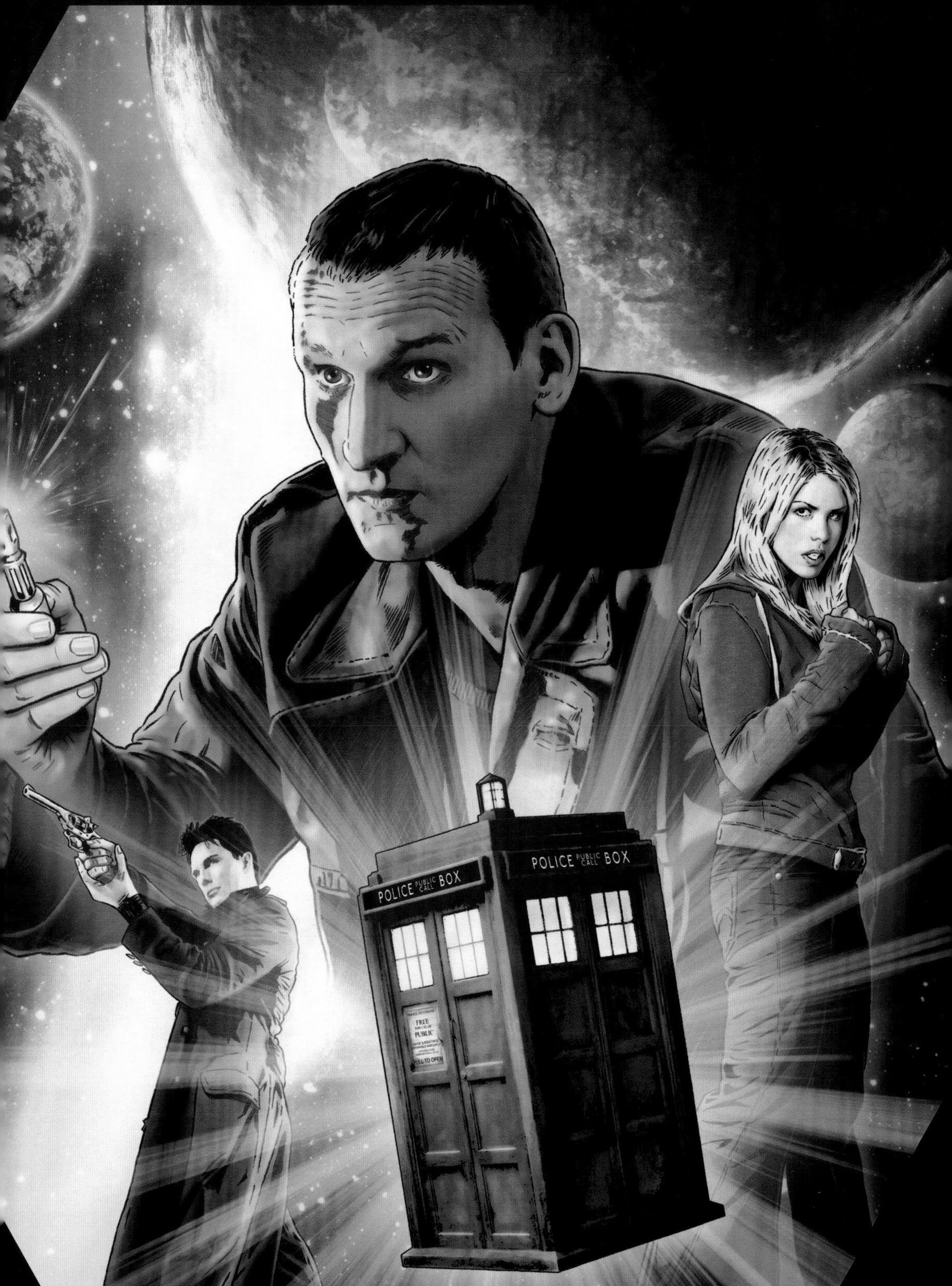
POLICE PUBLIC CALL BOX
POLICE PUBLIC CALL BOX
FREE
PUBLIC
PULL TO OPEN

9D #5 Cover C: JOE CORRONEY

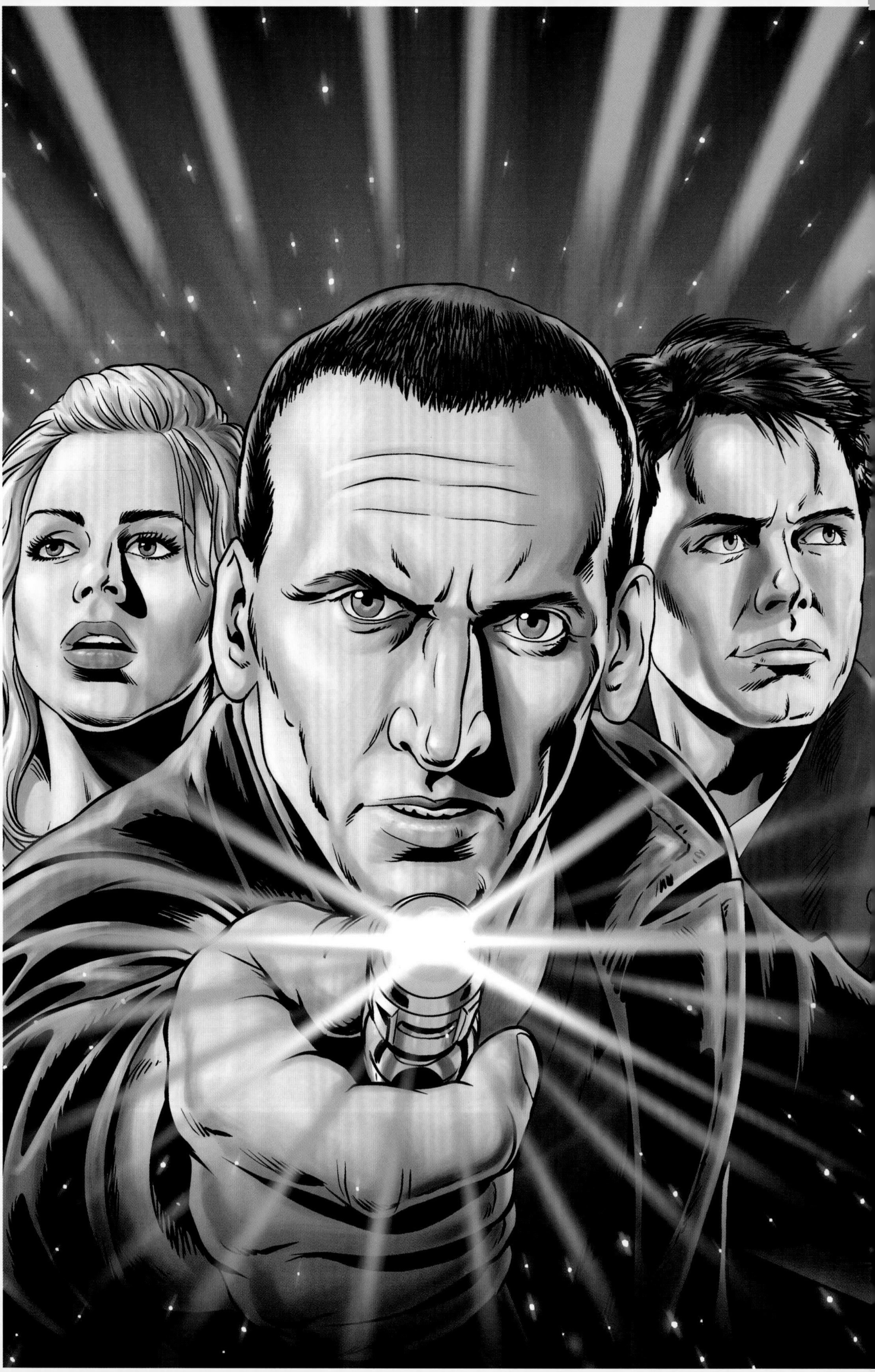

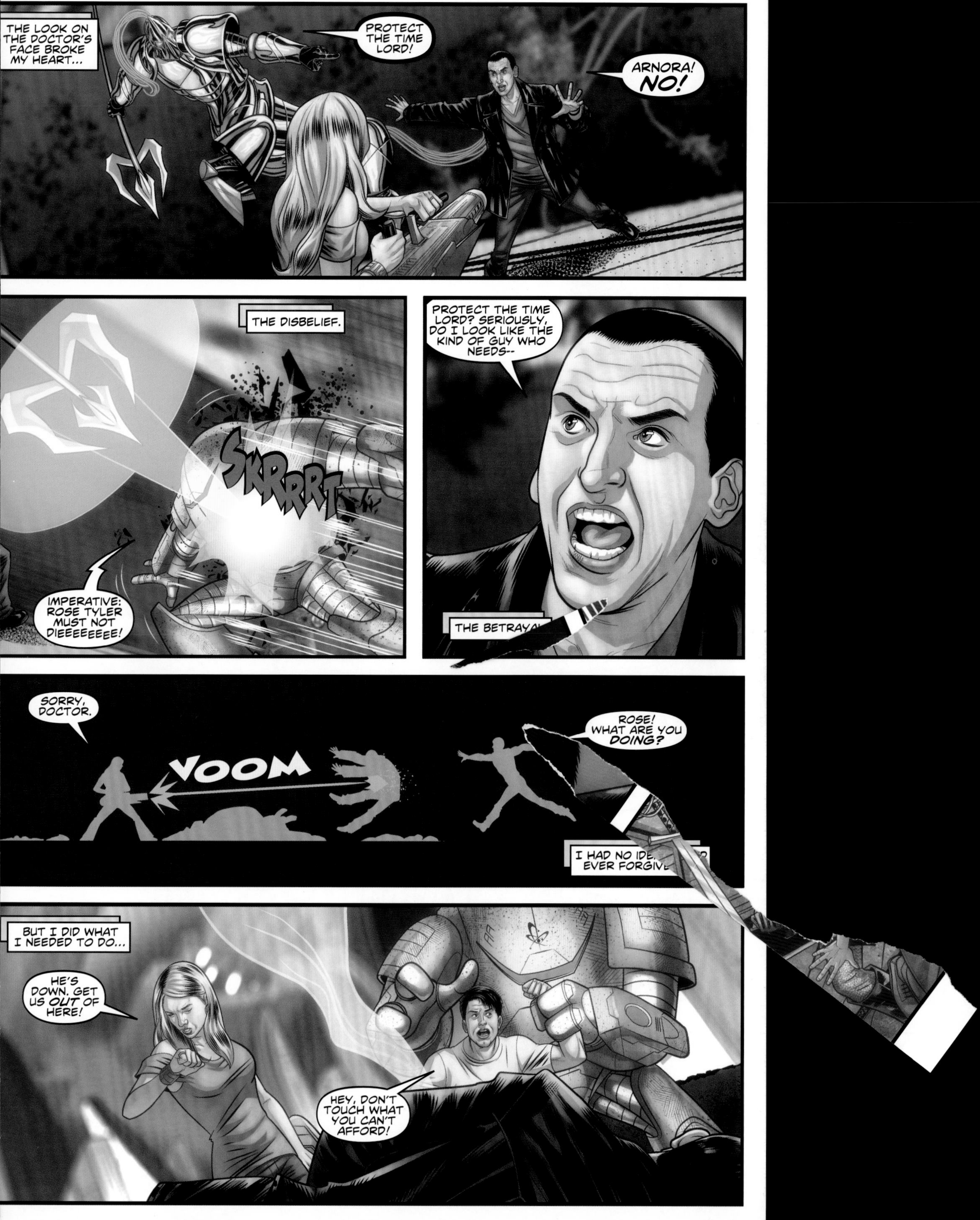
THE LOOK ON THE DOCTOR'S FACE BROKE MY HEART...
PROTECT THE TIME LORD!
ARNORA! NO!
THE DISBELIEF.
SKRRRT
IMPERATIVE: ROSE TYLER MUST NOT DIEEEEEEEE!
PROTECT THE TIME LORD? SERIOUSLY, DO I LOOK LIKE THE KIND OF GUY WHO NEEDS--
THE BETRAYA
SORRY, DOCTOR.
VOOM
ROSE! WHAT ARE YOU DOING?
I HAD NO IDE
EVER FORGIVE
BUT I DID WHAT I NEEDED TO DO...
HE'S DOWN. GET US OUT OF HERE!
HEY, DON'T TOUCH WHAT YOU CAN'T AFFORD!

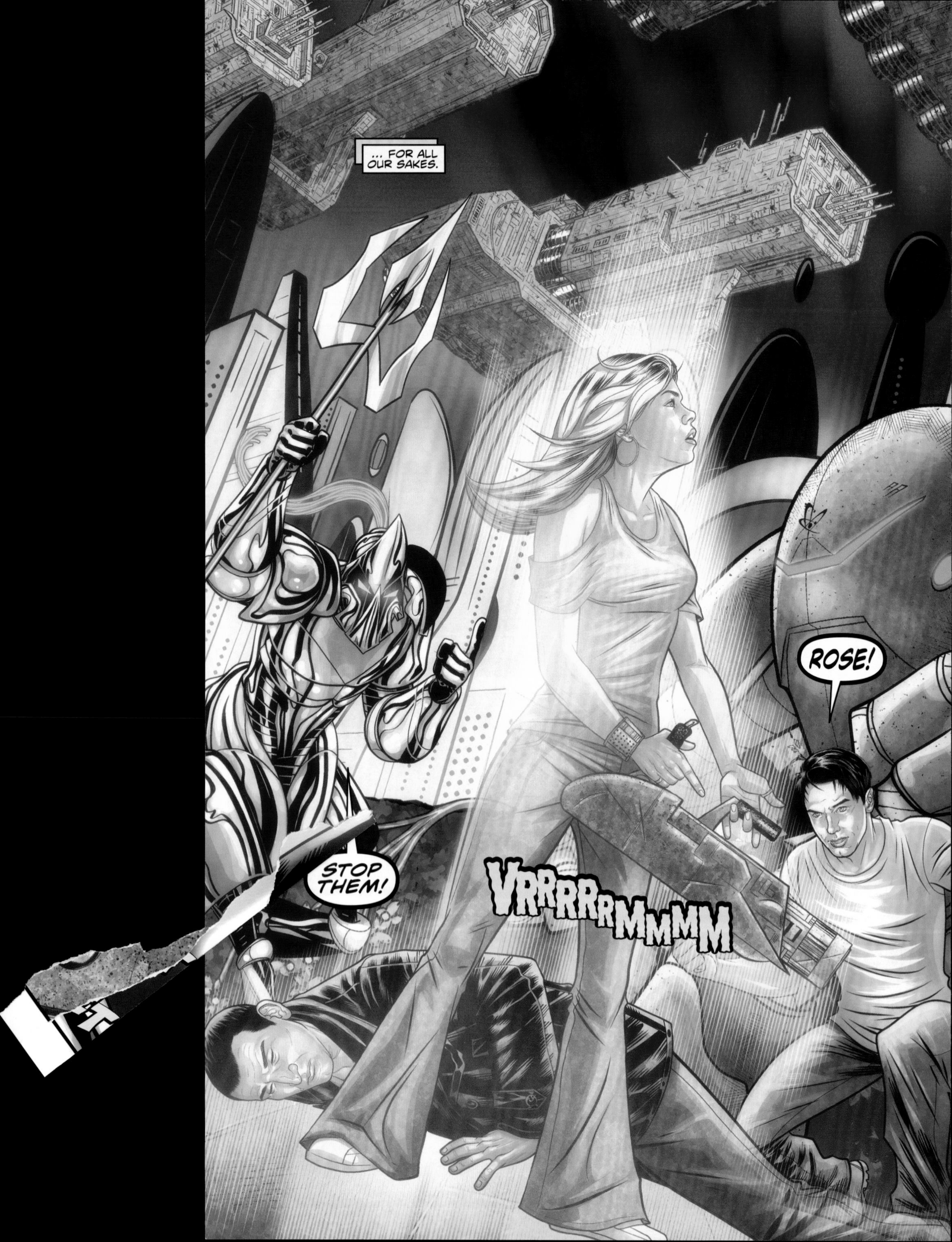

... FOR ALL OUR SAKES.
ROSE!
STOP THEM!
VRRRRRRMMMMM

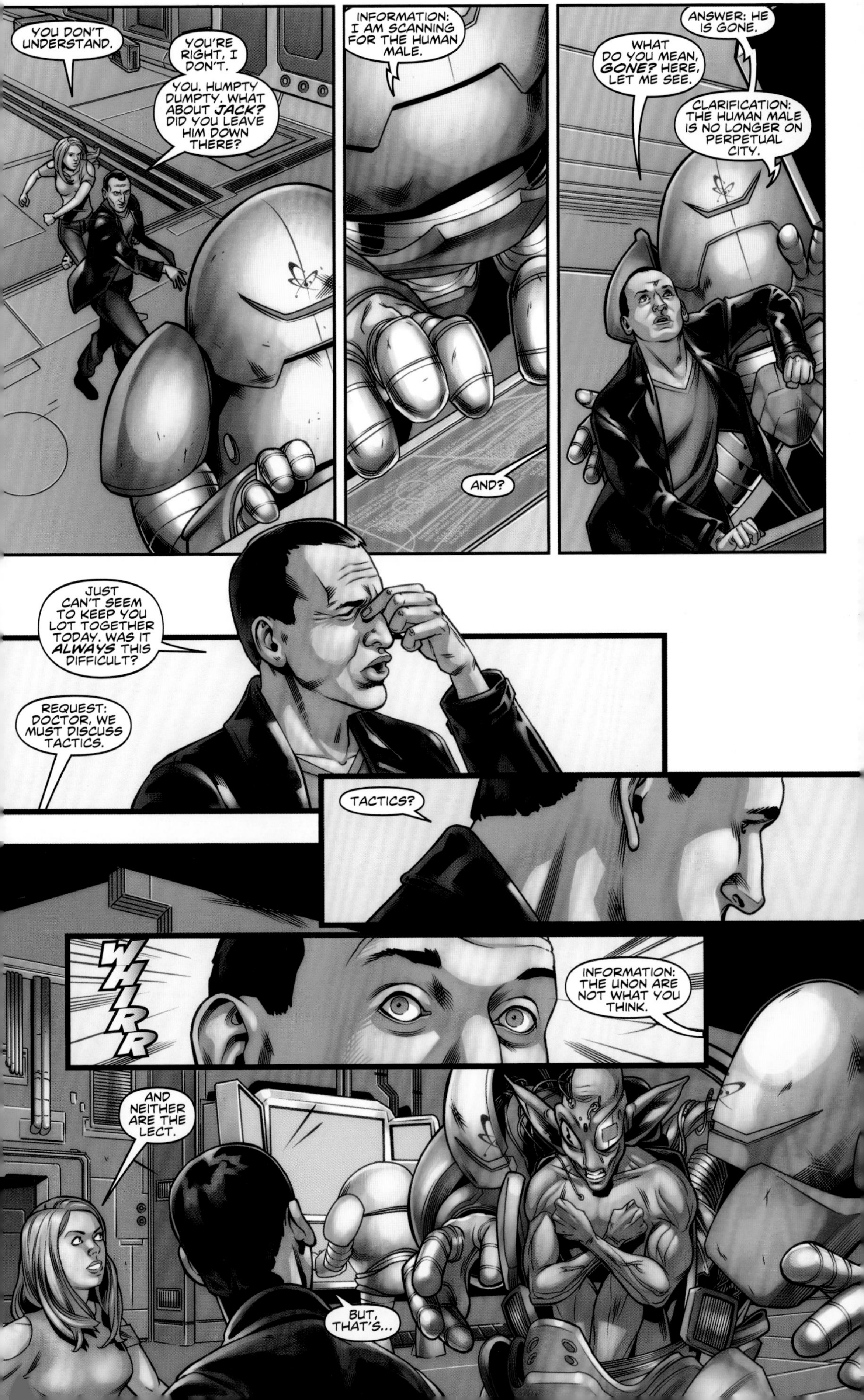
YOU DON'T UNDERSTAND.
YOU'RE RIGHT, I DON'T.
YOU. HUMPTY DUMPTY. WHAT ABOUT JACK? DID YOU LEAVE HIM DOWN THERE?
INFORMATION: I AM SCANNING FOR THE HUMAN MALE.
AND?
ANSWER: HE IS GONE.
WHAT DO YOU MEAN, GONE? HERE, LET ME SEE.
CLARIFICATION: THE HUMAN MALE IS NO LONGER ON PERPETUAL CITY.
JUST CAN'T SEEM TO KEEP YOU LOT TOGETHER TODAY. WAS IT ALWAYS THIS DIFFICULT?
REQUEST: DOCTOR, WE MUST DISCUSS TACTICS.
TACTICS?
WHIRR
INFORMATION: THE UNON ARE NOT WHAT YOU THINK.
AND NEITHER ARE THE LECT.
BUT, THAT'S...

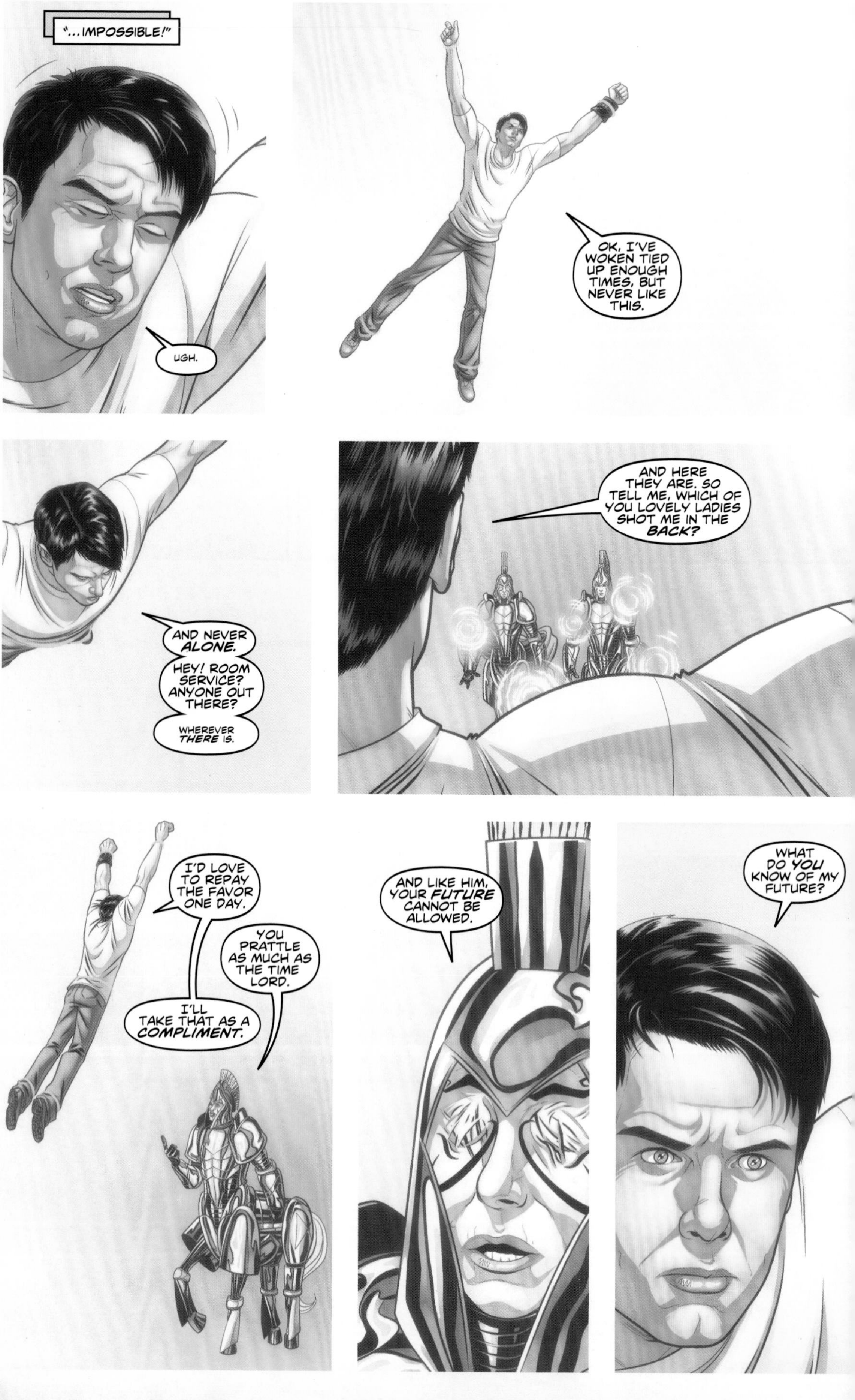
"...IMPOSSIBLE!"
UGH.
OK, I'VE WOKEN TIED UP ENOUGH TIMES, BUT NEVER LIKE THIS.
AND NEVER ALONE.
HEY! ROOM SERVICE? ANYONE OUT THERE?
WHEREVER THERE IS.
AND HERE THEY ARE. SO TELL ME, WHICH OF YOU LOVELY LADIES SHOT ME IN THE BACK?
I'D LOVE TO REPAY THE FAVOR ONE DAY.
YOU PRATTLE AS MUCH AS THE TIME LORD.
I'LL TAKE THAT AS A COMPLIMENT.
AND LIKE HIM, YOUR FUTURE CANNOT BE ALLOWED.
WHAT DO YOU KNOW OF MY FUTURE?

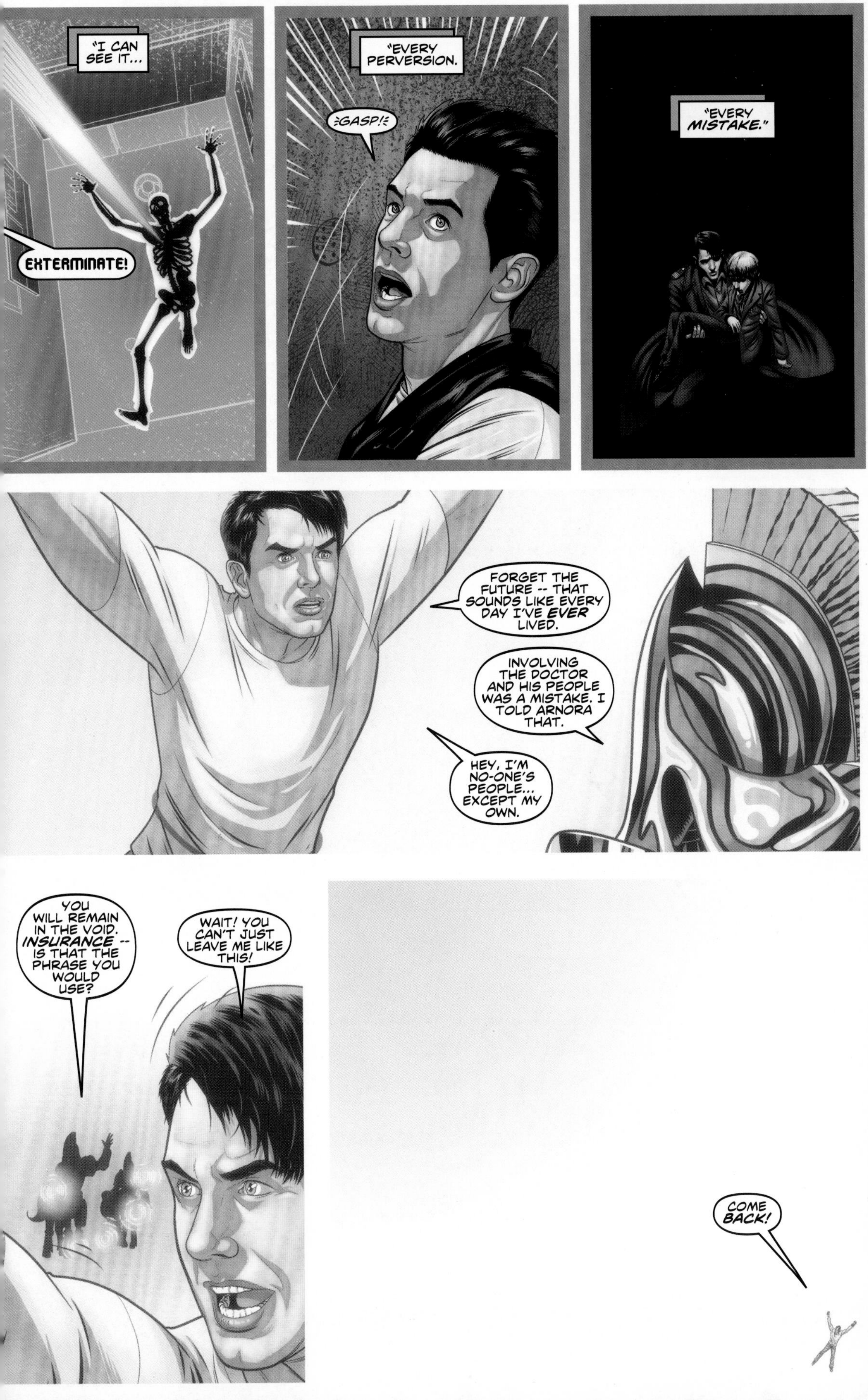
"I CAN SEE IT...
EXTERMINATE!
"EVERY PERVERSION.
GASP!
"EVERY MISTAKE."
FORGET THE FUTURE -- THAT SOUNDS LIKE EVERY DAY I'VE EVER LIVED.
INVOLVING THE DOCTOR AND HIS PEOPLE WAS A MISTAKE. I TOLD ARNORA THAT.
HEY, I'M NO-ONE'S PEOPLE... EXCEPT MY OWN.
YOU WILL REMAIN IN THE VOID. INSURANCE -- IS THAT THE PHRASE YOU WOULD USE?
WAIT! YOU CAN'T JUST LEAVE ME LIKE THIS!
COME BACK!

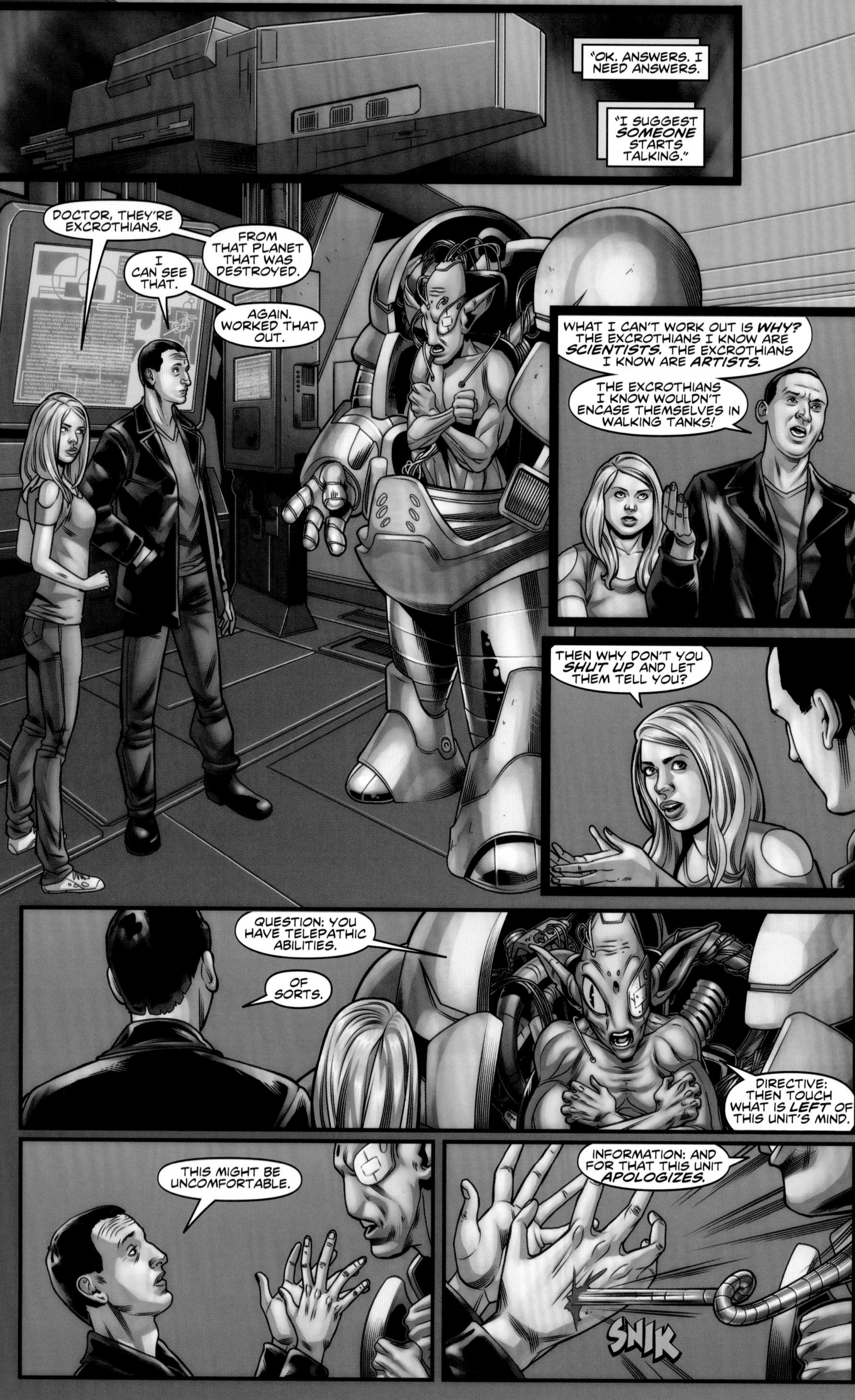
"OK. ANSWERS. I NEED ANSWERS.
"I SUGGEST SOMEONE STARTS TALKING."
DOCTOR, THEY'RE EXCROTHIANS.
I CAN SEE THAT.
FROM THAT PLANET THAT WAS DESTROYED.
AGAIN. WORKED THAT OUT.
WHAT I CAN'T WORK OUT IS WHY? THE EXCROTHIANS I KNOW ARE SCIENTISTS. THE EXCROTHIANS I KNOW ARE ARTISTS.
THE EXCROTHIANS I KNOW WOULDN'T ENCASE THEMSELVES IN WALKING TANKS!
THEN WHY DON'T YOU SHUT UP AND LET THEM TELL YOU?
QUESTION: YOU HAVE TELEPATHIC ABILITIES.
OF SORTS.
DIRECTIVE: THEN TOUCH WHAT IS LEFT OF THIS UNIT'S MIND.
THIS MIGHT BE UNCOMFORTABLE.
INFORMATION: AND FOR THAT THIS UNIT APOLOGIZES.
SNIK

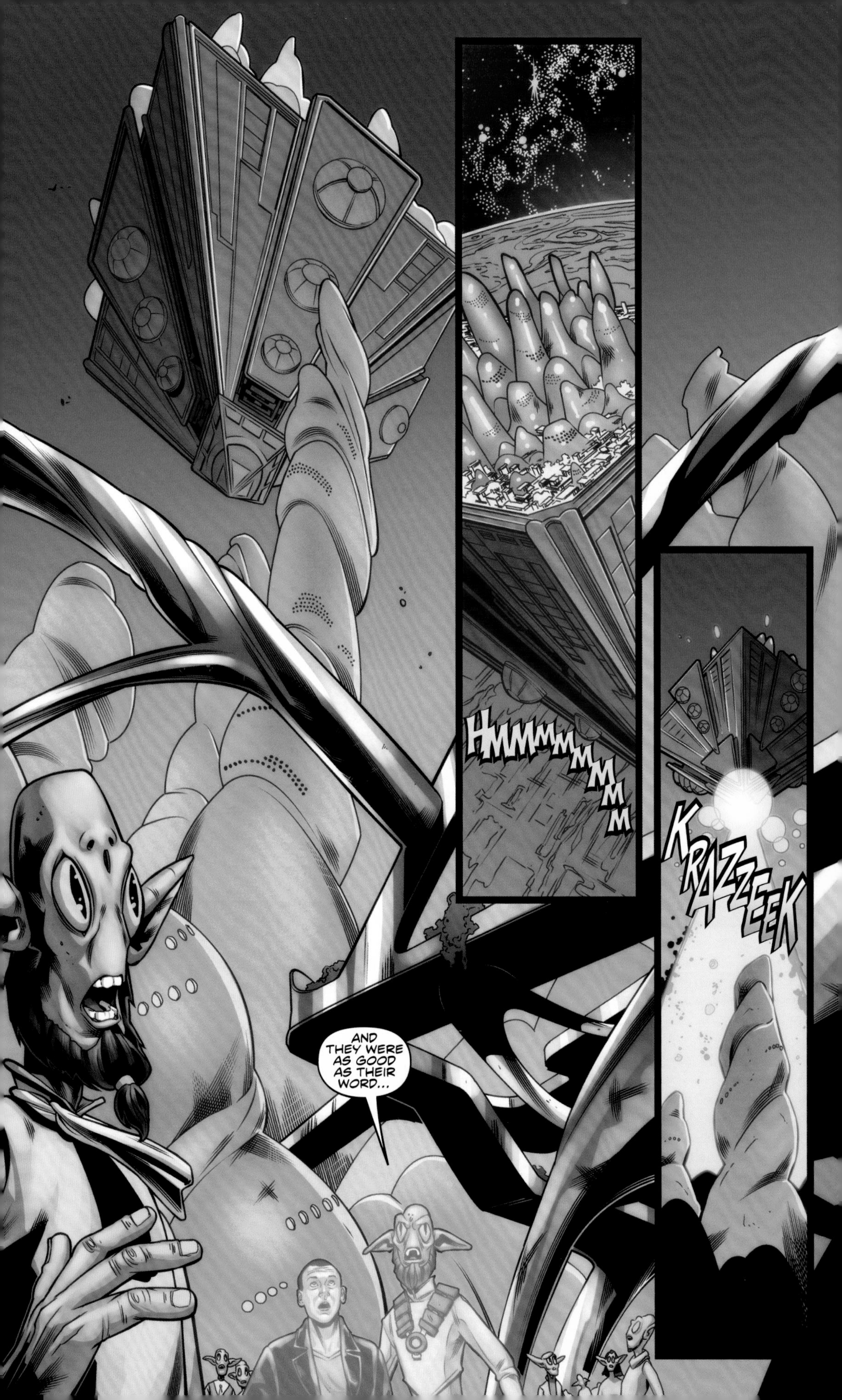
HMMMMMMMMM
KRAZZEEK
AND THEY WERE AS GOOD AS THEIR WORD...

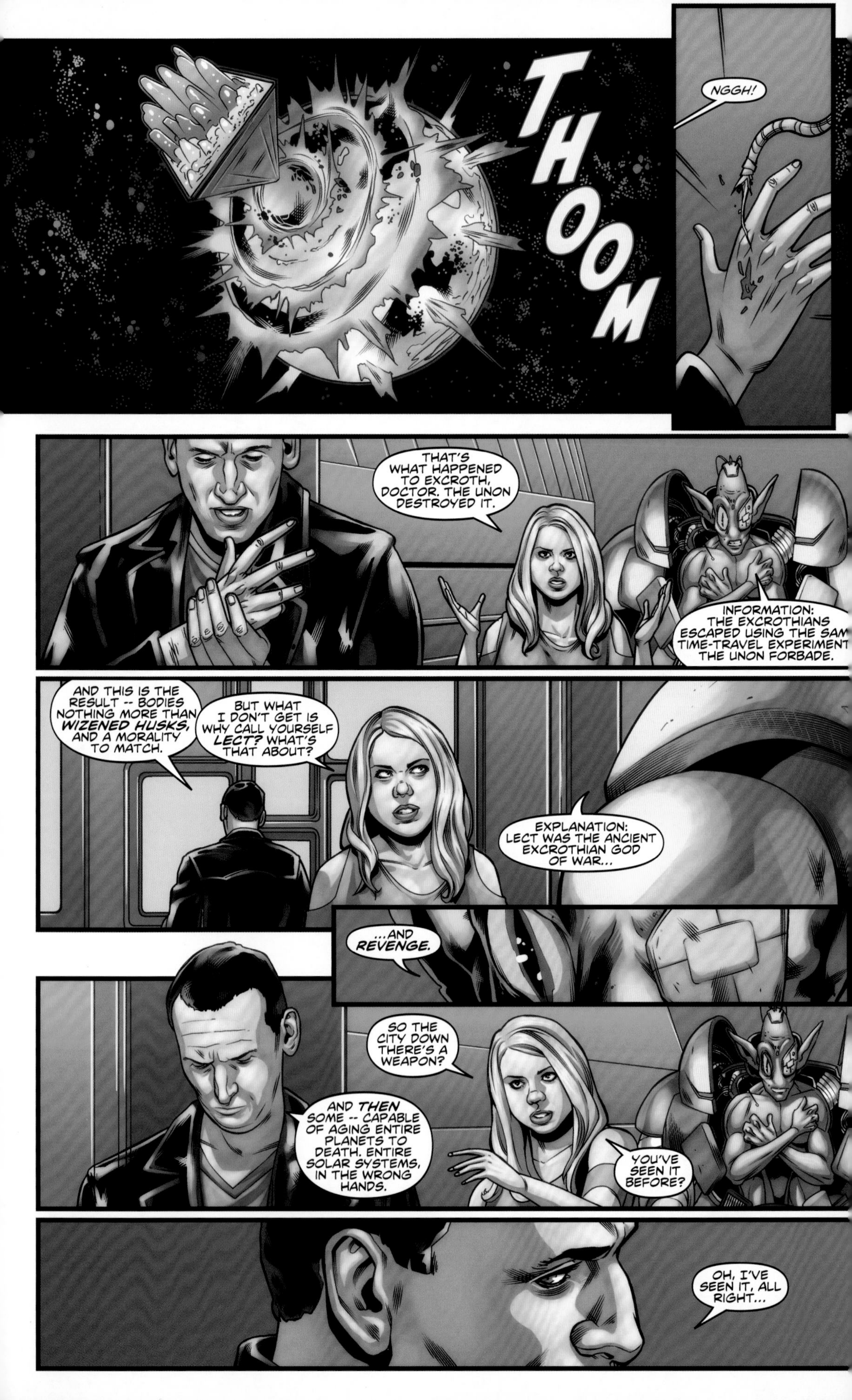
THOOM
NGGH!
THAT'S WHAT HAPPENED TO EXCROTH, DOCTOR. THE UNON DESTROYED IT.
INFORMATION: THE EXCROTHIANS ESCAPED USING THE SAM TIME-TRAVEL EXPERIMENT THE UNON FORBADE.
AND THIS IS THE RESULT -- BODIES NOTHING MORE THAN WIZENED HUSKS, AND A MORALITY TO MATCH.
BUT WHAT I DON'T GET IS WHY CALL YOURSELF LECT? WHAT'S THAT ABOUT?
EXPLANATION: LECT WAS THE ANCIENT EXCROTHIAN GOD OF WAR...
...AND REVENGE.
SO THE CITY DOWN THERE'S A WEAPON?
AND THEN SOME -- CAPABLE OF AGING ENTIRE PLANETS TO DEATH. ENTIRE SOLAR SYSTEMS, IN THE WRONG HANDS.
YOU'VE SEEN IT BEFORE?
OH, I'VE SEEN IT, ALL RIGHT...

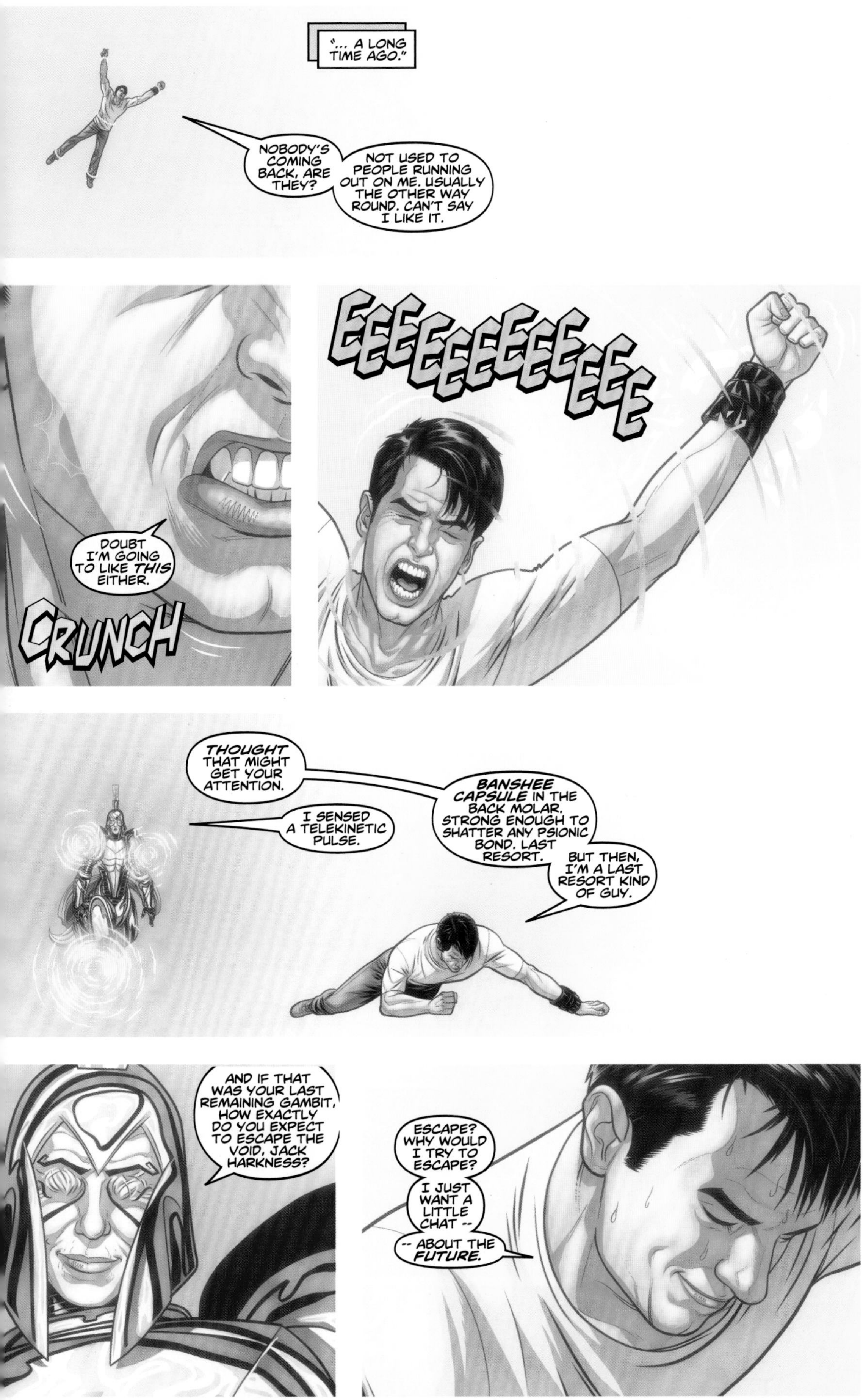
"... A LONG TIME AGO."
NOBODY'S COMING BACK, ARE THEY?
NOT USED TO PEOPLE RUNNING OUT ON ME. USUALLY THE OTHER WAY ROUND. CAN'T SAY I LIKE IT.
DOUBT I'M GOING TO LIKE *THIS* EITHER.
CRUNCH
EEEEEEEEEEEEE
THOUGHT THAT MIGHT GET YOUR ATTENTION.
I SENSED A TELEKINETIC PULSE.
BANSHEE CAPSULE IN THE BACK MOLAR. STRONG ENOUGH TO SHATTER ANY PSIONIC BOND. LAST RESORT.
BUT THEN, I'M A LAST RESORT KIND OF GUY.
AND IF THAT WAS YOUR LAST REMAINING GAMBIT, HOW EXACTLY DO YOU EXPECT TO ESCAPE THE VOID, JACK HARKNESS?
ESCAPE? WHY WOULD I TRY TO ESCAPE?
I JUST WANT A LITTLE CHAT --
-- ABOUT THE *FUTURE.*

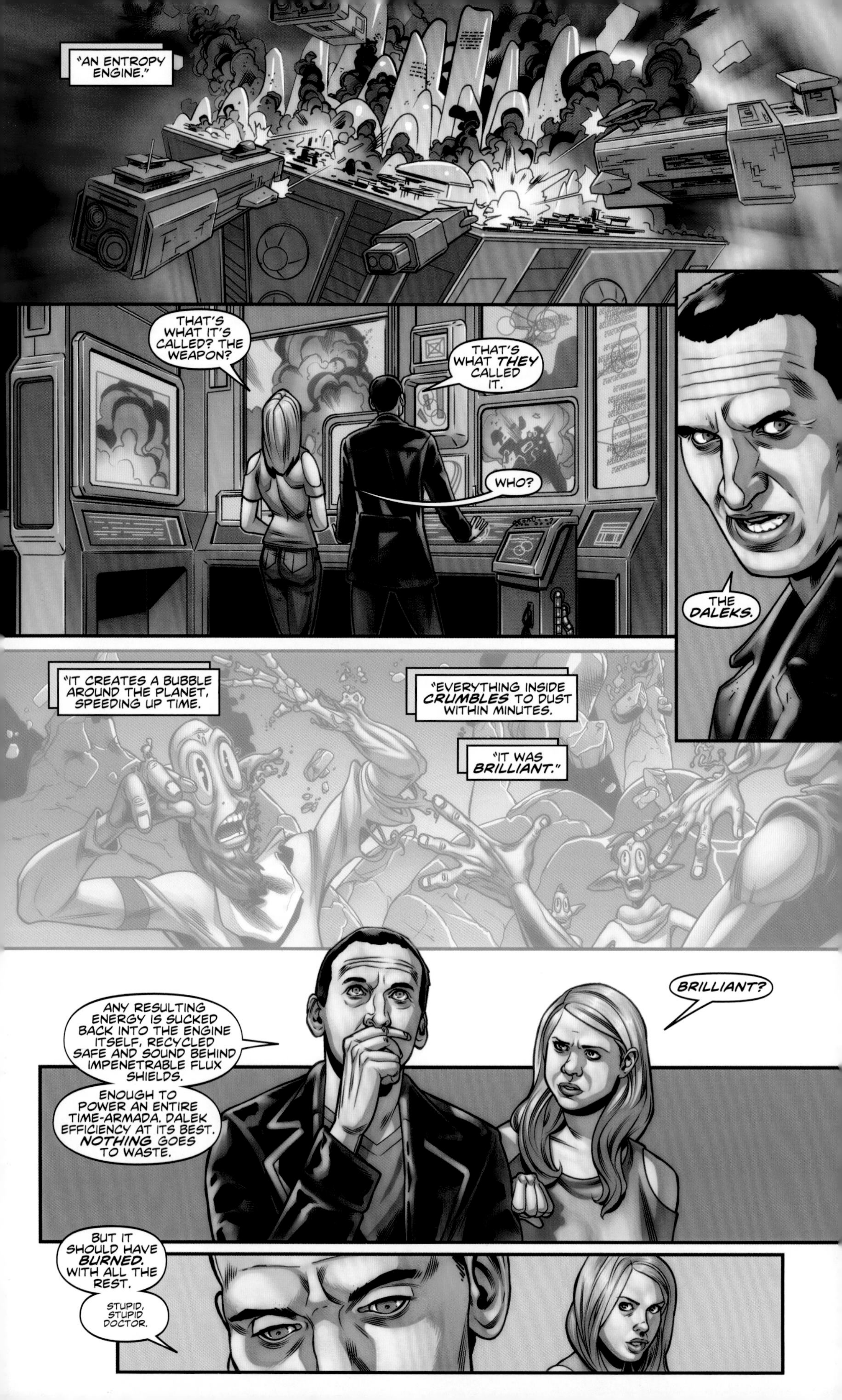

"AN ENTROPY ENGINE."
THAT'S WHAT IT'S CALLED? THE WEAPON?
THAT'S WHAT *THEY* CALLED IT.
WHO?
THE *DALEKS.*
"IT CREATES A BUBBLE AROUND THE PLANET, SPEEDING UP TIME.
"EVERYTHING INSIDE *CRUMBLES* TO DUST WITHIN MINUTES.
"IT WAS *BRILLIANT.*"
ANY RESULTING ENERGY IS SUCKED BACK INTO THE ENGINE ITSELF, RECYCLED SAFE AND SOUND BEHIND IMPENETRABLE FLUX SHIELDS.
ENOUGH TO POWER AN ENTIRE TIME-ARMADA. DALEK EFFICIENCY AT ITS BEST. *NOTHING* GOES TO WASTE.
BRILLIANT?
BUT IT SHOULD HAVE *BURNED.* WITH ALL THE REST.
STUPID, STUPID DOCTOR.

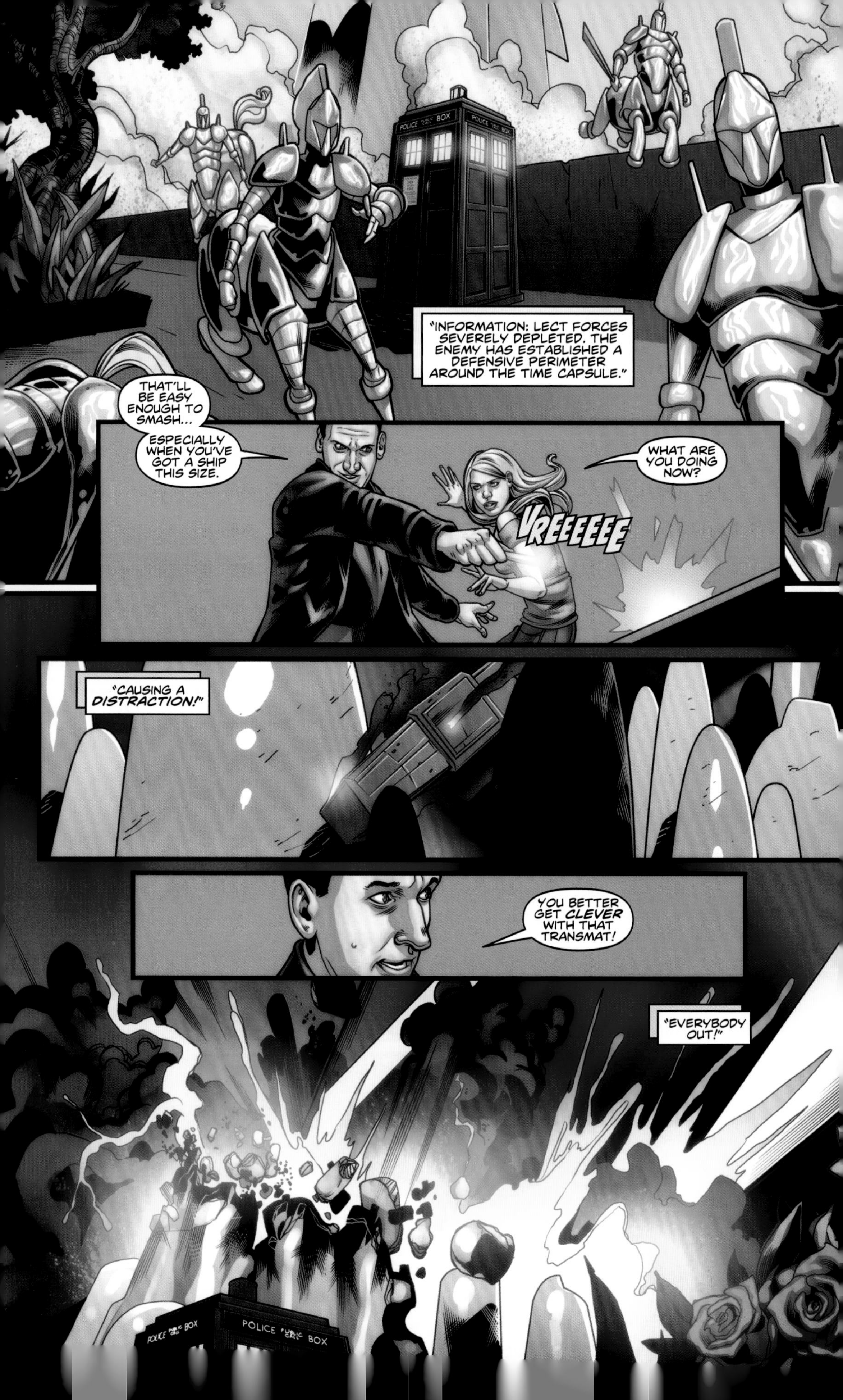
"INFORMATION: LECT FORCES SEVERELY DEPLETED. THE ENEMY HAS ESTABLISHED A DEFENSIVE PERIMETER AROUND THE TIME CAPSULE."
THAT'LL BE EASY ENOUGH TO SMASH...
ESPECIALLY WHEN YOU'VE GOT A SHIP THIS SIZE.
WHAT ARE YOU DOING NOW?
VREEEEEE
"CAUSING A DISTRACTION!"
YOU BETTER GET CLEVER WITH THAT TRANSMAT!
"EVERYBODY OUT!"
POLICE BOX
POLICE BOX

THERE SHE IS.

THAT WAS A LITTLE *EXTREME*, WASN'T IT?

MEANS TO AN END.

AND THAT MAKES IT ALL RIGHT?

"*NOTHING* ABOUT THIS IS ALL RIGHT."

NO!

VWORP

"WHICH IS WHY WE HAVE *WORK* TO DO."

OR RATHER *HE* DOES.

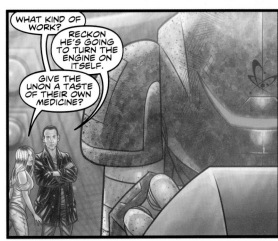

WHAT KIND OF WORK?

RECKON HE'S GOING TO TURN THE ENGINE ON ITSELF.

GIVE THE UNON A TASTE OF THEIR OWN MEDICINE?

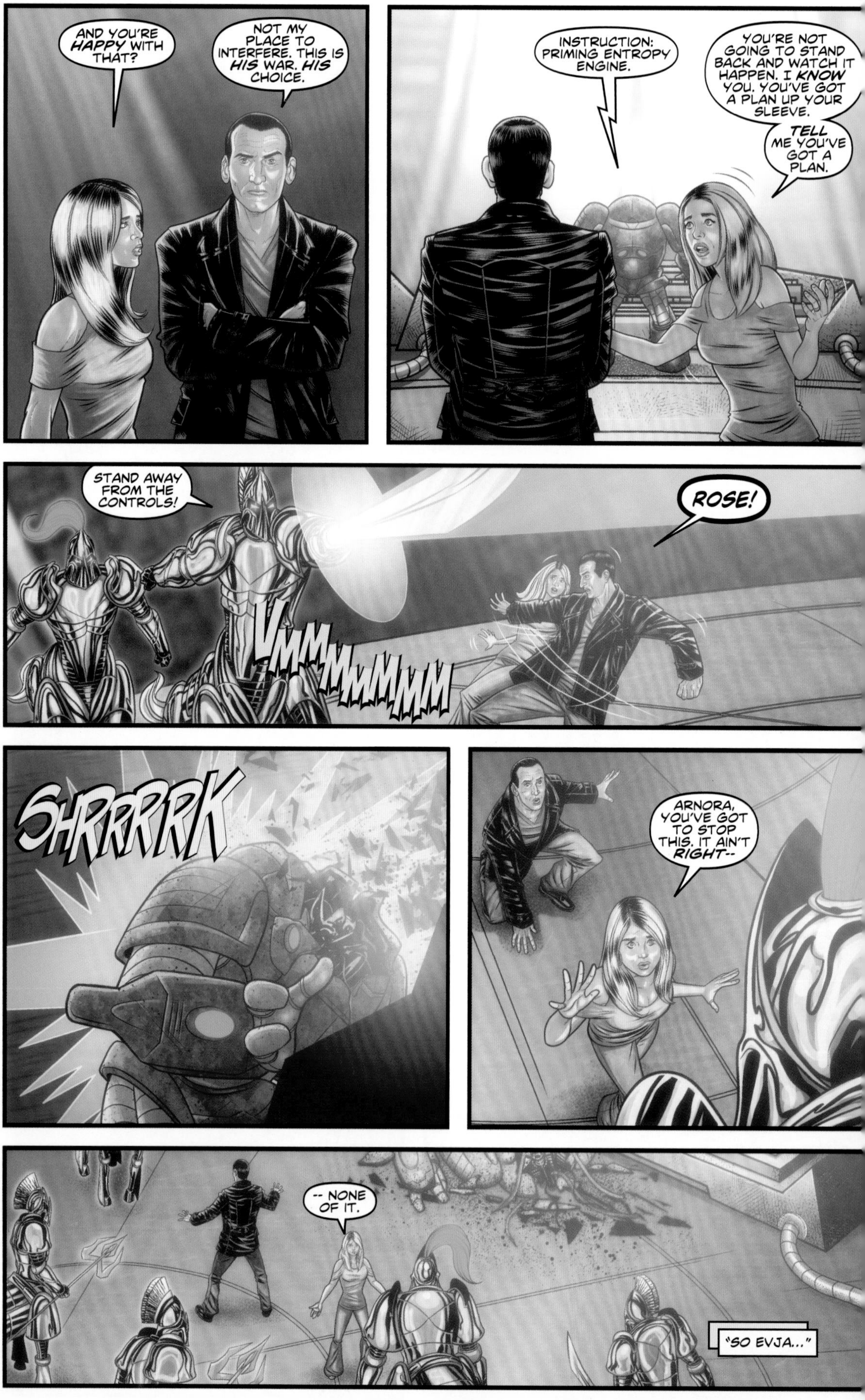
AND YOU'RE HAPPY WITH THAT?
NOT MY PLACE TO INTERFERE. THIS IS HIS WAR. HIS CHOICE.
INSTRUCTION: PRIMING ENTROPY ENGINE.
YOU'RE NOT GOING TO STAND BACK AND WATCH IT HAPPEN. I KNOW YOU. YOU'VE GOT A PLAN UP YOUR SLEEVE.
TELL ME YOU'VE GOT A PLAN.
STAND AWAY FROM THE CONTROLS!
ROSE!
VMMMMMMMM
SHRRRRK
ARNORA, YOU'VE GOT TO STOP THIS. IT AIN'T RIGHT--
-- NONE OF IT.
"SO EVJA..."

...YOU *SAY* YOU CAN SEE THE DOCTOR'S FUTURE.

I SEE THE ROAD HE TRAVELS. THE SAME ROAD HE HAS *ALWAYS* TRAVELED. THE DOCTOR IS AN ANGEL OF DEATH. CHAOS CLINGS TO HIM LIKE AN OLD LOVER. WHERE HE GOES, *DESTRUCTION* FOLLOWS.

FUNNY...

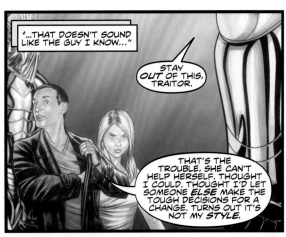

"...THAT DOESN'T SOUND LIKE THE GUY I KNOW..."

STAY *OUT* OF THIS, TRAITOR.

THAT'S THE TROUBLE, SHE CAN'T HELP HERSELF. THOUGHT I COULD. THOUGHT I'D LET SOMEONE *ELSE* MAKE THE TOUGH DECISIONS FOR A CHANGE. TURNS OUT IT'S NOT MY *STYLE*.

SO HERE'S *YOUR* CHOICE, ARNORA. STAND DOWN, OR I'LL IGNITE THE ENGINE. SIMPLE AS THAT.

"THE THING IS, HAVE YOU TRIED LOOKING FOR A FUTURE *WITHOUT* HIM?"

YOU WOULDN'T DARE.

WHY NOT? I'VE DONE IT BEFORE.

"A FUTURE WITH ONLY THE *UNON* IN CHARGE."

YOU WANTED TO REPLACE THE TIME LORDS. FILL THEIR SHOES. AND DO YOU KNOW WHAT?

PARANOIA? CHECK.

CORRUPTION? NOT A PROBLEM.

TYRANNY? JOB DONE.

"TELL ME, EVJA..."

CONGRATULATIONS. YOU'RE THE IDEAL CANDIDATES.

"... HOW DOES THAT WORK OUT?"

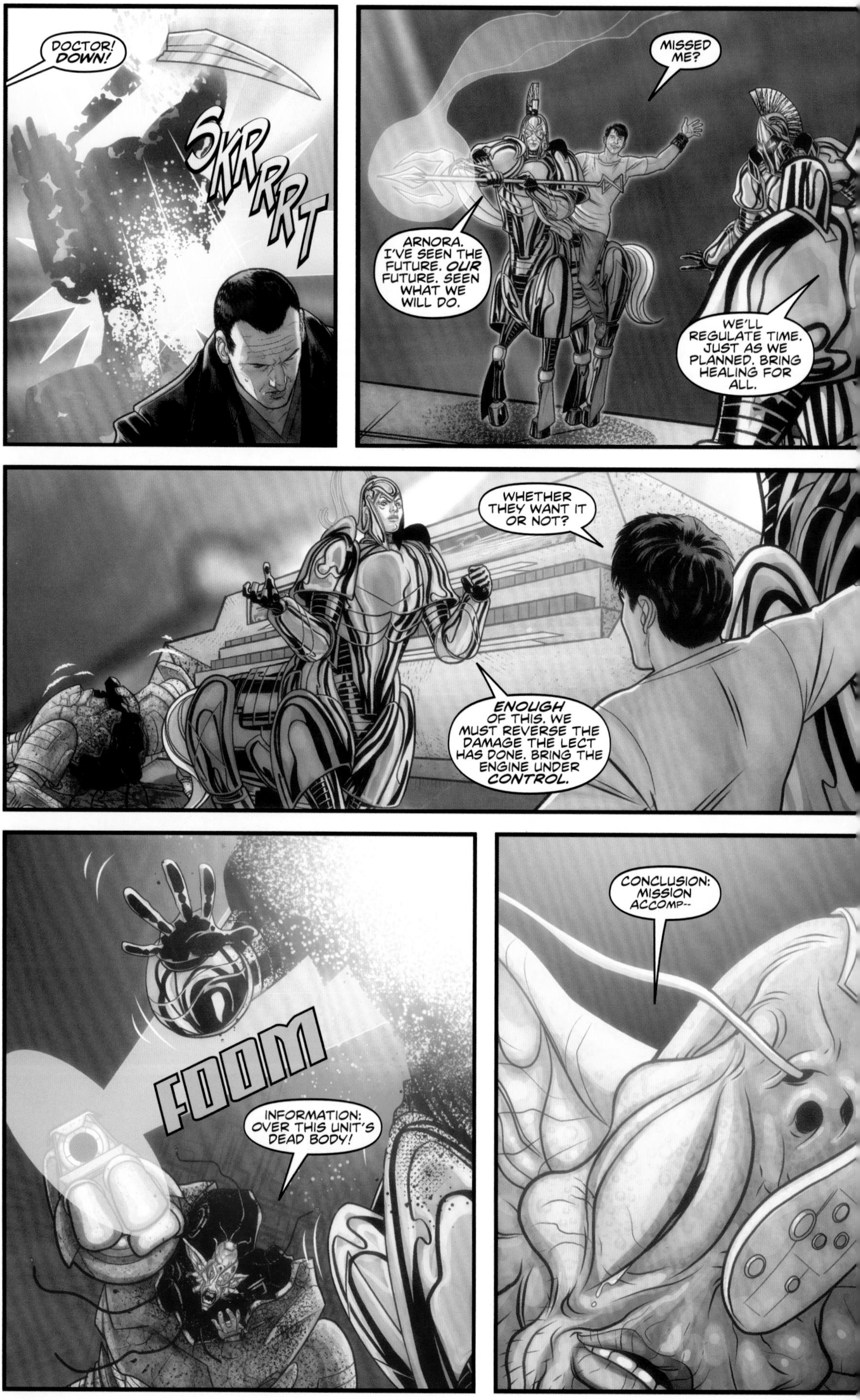
DOCTOR! DOWN!
SKRRRRT
MISSED ME?
ARNORA. I'VE SEEN THE FUTURE. OUR FUTURE. SEEN WHAT WE WILL DO.
WE'LL REGULATE TIME. JUST AS WE PLANNED. BRING HEALING FOR ALL.
WHETHER THEY WANT IT OR NOT?
ENOUGH OF THIS. WE MUST REVERSE THE DAMAGE THE LECT HAS DONE. BRING THE ENGINE UNDER CONTROL.
FOOM
INFORMATION: OVER THIS UNIT'S DEAD BODY!
CONCLUSION: MISSION ACCOMP--

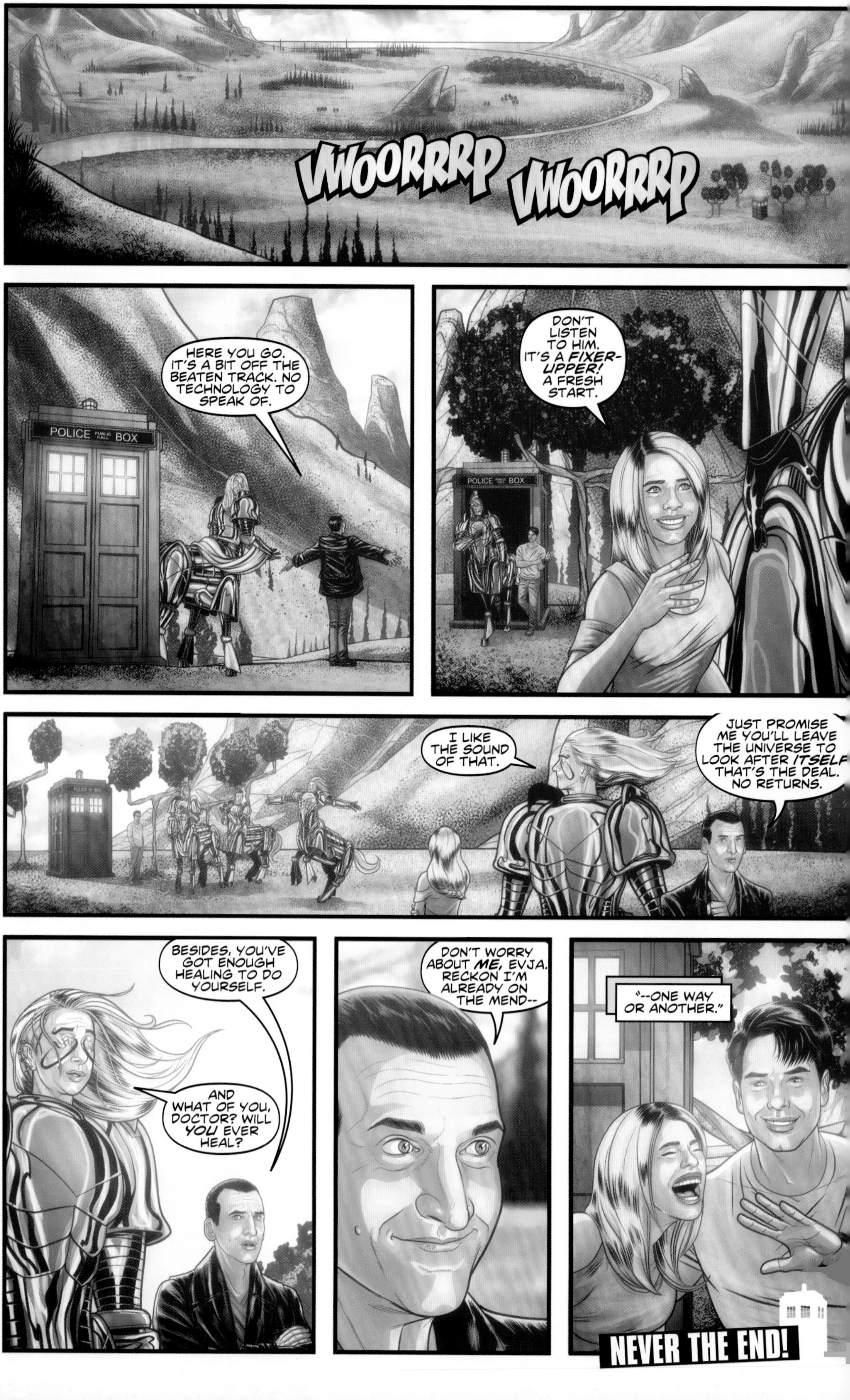

VWOORRRP VWOORRRP
HERE YOU GO. IT'S A BIT OFF THE BEATEN TRACK. NO TECHNOLOGY TO SPEAK OF.
POLICE PUBLIC CALL BOX
DON'T LISTEN TO HIM. IT'S A FIXER-UPPER! A FRESH START.
I LIKE THE SOUND OF THAT.
JUST PROMISE ME YOU'LL LEAVE THE UNIVERSE TO LOOK AFTER ITSELF. THAT'S THE DEAL. NO RETURNS.
BESIDES, YOU'VE GOT ENOUGH HEALING TO DO YOURSELF.
AND WHAT OF YOU, DOCTOR? WILL YOU EVER HEAL?
DON'T WORRY ABOUT ME, EVJA. RECKON I'M ALREADY ON THE MEND--
"--ONE WAY OR ANOTHER."
NEVER THE END!

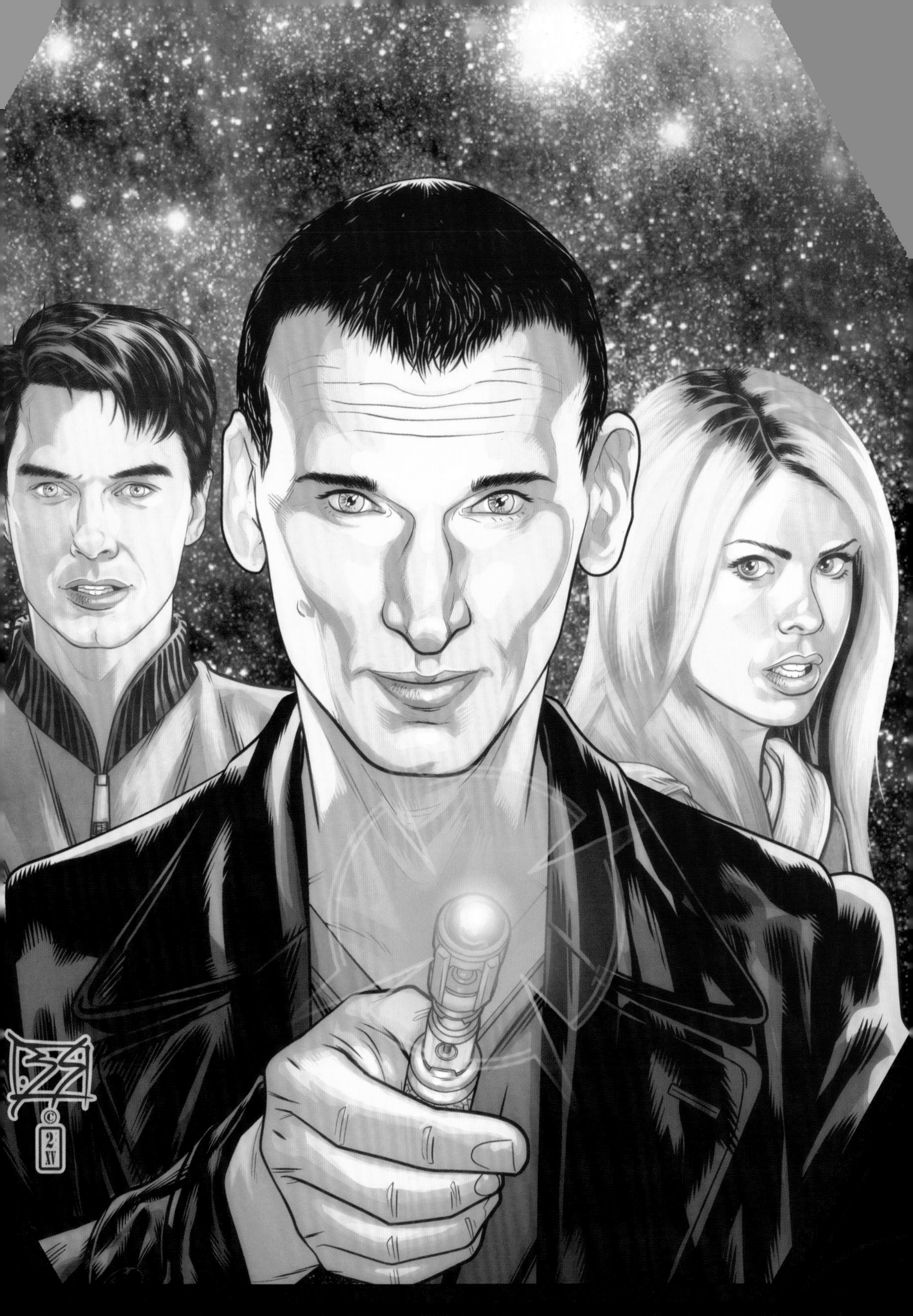

9D #1 Newbury Comics Cover: BLAIR SHEDD

DOCTOR WHO
THE NINTH DOCTOR

COVER GALLERY

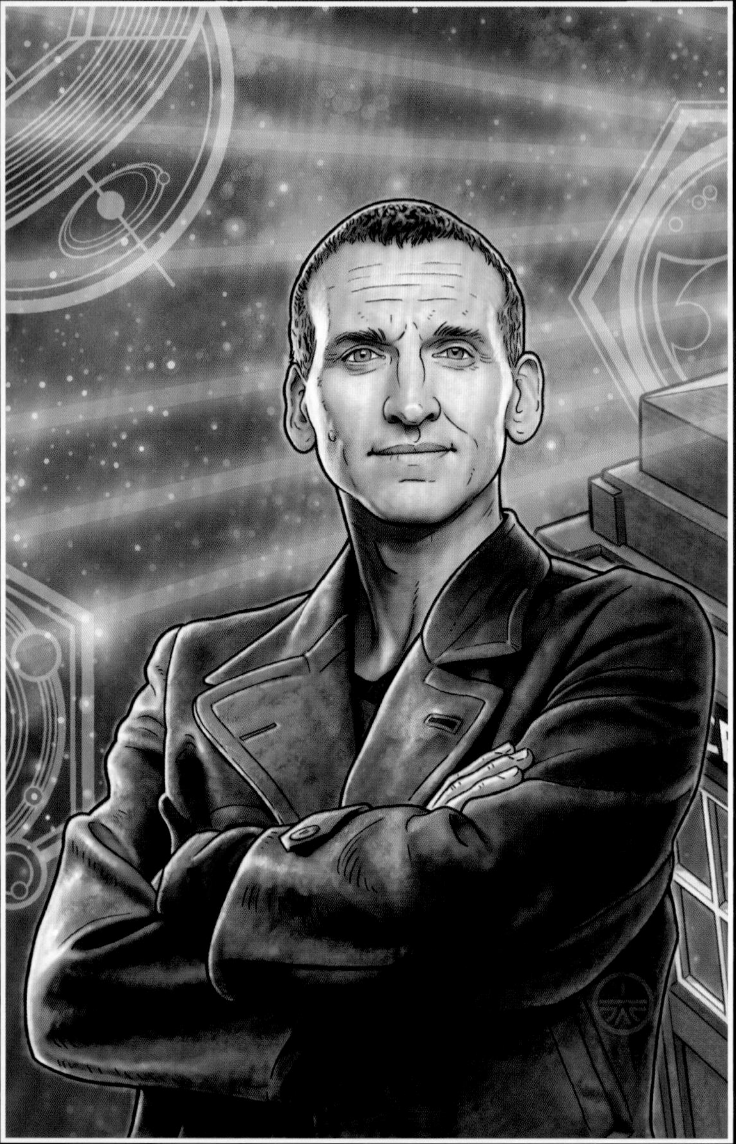

A

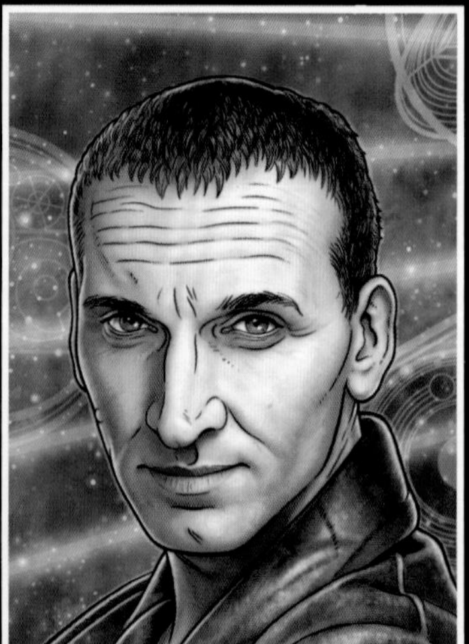

B

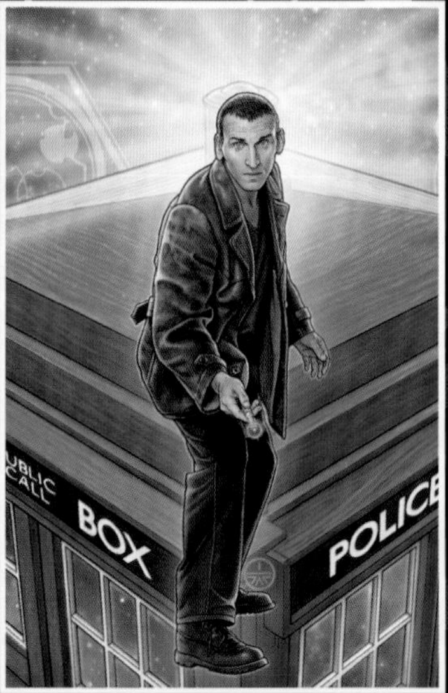
BOX
POLICE

C

ISSUES #1 - 3

A: #2 Hastings Cover – JEFF CARLISLE
B: #1 Hastings Cover – JEFF CARLISLE
C: #3 Hastings Cover – JEFF CARLISLE

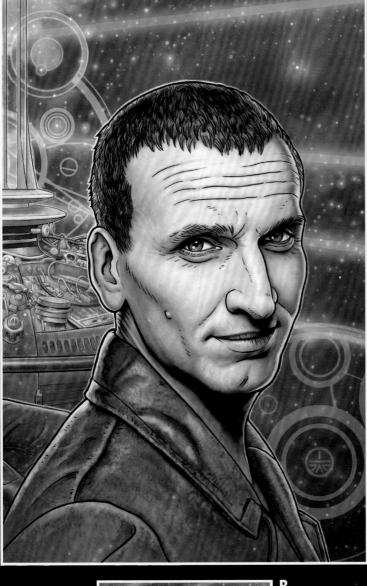

BBC DOCTOR WHO THE NINTH DOCTOR

COVER GALLERY

A

B

PUBLIC CALL

ISSUES #4 - 5

A: #5 Hastings Cover – JEFF CARLISLE
B: #4 Hastings Cover – JEFF CARLISLE

FOLLOW YOUR FAVORITE INCARNATIONS ACROSS THESE FANTASTIC COLLECTIONS!

DOCTOR WHO: THE TENTH DOCTOR
VOL. 1: REVOLUTIONS OF TERROR

BBC NEW ADVENTURES WITH THE TENTH DOCTOR
DOCTOR WHO
REVOLUTIONS OF TERROR
NICK ABADZIS • ELENA CASAGRANDE • ARIANNA FLOREAN

ISBN: 9781782761747
ON SALE NOW - $19.99 / $22.95 CAN / £10.99
(UK EDITION ISBN: 9781782763840)

DOCTOR WHO: THE TENTH DOCTOR
VOL. 2: THE WEEPING ANGELS OF MONS

BBC NEW ADVENTURES WITH THE TENTH DOCTOR
DOCTOR WHO
THE WEEPING ANGELS OF MONS
ROBBIE MORRISON • DANIEL INDRO • SLAMET MUJIONO

ISBN: 9781782761754
ON SALE NOW - $19.99 / $25.99 CAN / £10.99
(UK EDITION ISBN: 9781782766575)

DOCTOR WHO: THE TENTH DOCTOR
VOL. 3:THE FOUNTAINS OF FOREVER

BBC NEW ADVENTURES WITH THE TENTH DOCTOR
DOCTOR WHO
THE FOUNTAINS OF FOREVER
NICK ABADZIS • ELENA CASAGRANDE
ELEONORA CARLINI • ARIANNA FLOREAN

ISBN: 9781782763024
COMING SOON - $19.99 / $25.99 CAN / £10.99
(UK EDITION ISBN: 9781782767404)

DOCTOR WHO: THE ELEVENTH DOCTOR
VOL. 1: AFTER LIFE

BBC NEW ADVENTURES WITH THE ELEVENTH DOCTOR
DOCTOR WHO
AFTER LIFE
AL EWING • ROB WILLIAMS • SIMON FRASER • BOO COOK
GARY CALDWELL • HI-FI

ISBN: 9781782761730
ON SALE NOW - $19.99 / $22.95 CAN / £10.99
(UK EDITION ISBN: 9781782763857)

DOCTOR WHO: THE ELEVENTH DOCTOR
VOL. 2: SERVE YOU

BBC NEW ADVENTURES WITH THE ELEVENTH DOCTOR
DOCTOR WHO
SERVE YOU
AL EWING • ROB WILLIAMS • SIMON FRASER • BOO COOK • WARREN PLEECE
GARY CALDWELL • HI-FI

ISBN: 9781782761754
ON SALE NOW - $19.99 / $22.95 CAN / £10.99
(UK EDITION ISBN: 9781782766582)

DOCTOR WHO: THE ELEVENTH DOCTOR
VOL. 3: CONVERSION

BBC NEW ADVENTURES WITH THE ELEVENTH DOCTOR
DOCTOR WHO
CONVERSION
AL EWING • ROB WILLIAMS • SIMON FRASER • BOO COOK • WARREN PLEECE
GARY CALDWELL • HI-FI

ISBN: 9781782763024
COMING SOON - $19.99 / $25.99 CAN / £10.99
(UK EDITION ISBN: 9781782767435)

TITAN COMICS

For information on how to subscribe to our great Doctor Who titles, or to purchase them digitally, visit:

WWW.TITAN-COMICS.COM

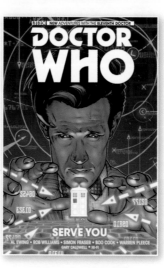

COMPLETE YOUR COLLECTION!

**DOCTOR WHO: THE TWELFTH DOCTOR
VOL. 1: TERRORFORMER**

ISBN: 9781782761778
ON SALE NOW - $19.99 / $22.95 CAN / £10.99
(UK EDITION ISBN: 9781782763864)

**DOCTOR WHO: THE TWELFTH DOCTOR
VOL. 2: FRACTURES**

ISBN: 9781782763017
ON SALE NOW - $19.99 / $25.99 CAN / £10.99
(UK EDITION ISBN: 9781782766599)

**DOCTOR WHO: THE TWELFTH DOCTOR
VOL. 3: HYPERION**

ISBN: 9781782767473
COMING SOON - $19.99 / $25.99 CAN / £10.99
(UK EDITION ISBN: 97817827674442)

**DOCTOR WHO: THE EIGHTH DOCTOR
VOL. 1: A MATTER OF LIFE AND DEATH**

ISBN: 9781782767534
COMING SOON - $19.99 / $25.99 CAN / £10.99
(UK EDITION ISBN: 9781785852855)

**DOCTOR WHO EVENT:
FOUR DOCTORS**

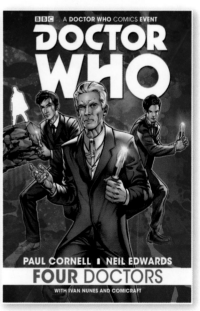

ISBN: 9781782765967
ON SALE NOW - $19.99 / $25.99 CAN / £10.99
(UK EDITION ISBN: 9781785851063)

AVAILABLE FROM ALL GOOD COMIC STORES, BOOK STORES, AND DIGITAL PROVIDERS!

BIOGRAPHIES

Cavan Scott is a writer, editor and journalist. He is known for his comics writing on *Doctor Who: The Twelfth Doctor*, *Adventure Time* and *Power Rangers,* as well as his many novels, including the upcoming *Sherlock Holmes* and *Star Wars: Adventures in Wild Space* novels. He is also known for co-writing the bestselling *Who-Ology* book. He has written for over thirty magazines in the UK, and founded the award-winning *Countryfile Magazine.* He lives in Bristol with his wife, two daughters and an inflatable Dalek named Desmond.

Blair Shedd is an Amerian comic book artist who was educated at the Kubert school under Joe Kubert himself, subsequently forming oneGemini studios. An artist and writer, he has illustrated *Ghostbusters, Legends of Oz: Dorothy's Return, The Guild,* and many more. He lives in New England with his wife and three kids.

Rachael Stott is a comic book artist and illustrator based in London. As well as illustrating *Doctor Who* (becoming the new regular artist on the *Twelfth Doctor* ongoing series from January 2016), she has drawn *Star Trek* and the *Star Trek/ Planet of the Apes* crossover. She won the Best Newcomer Prize at the 2015 British Comic Awards.

Anang Setyawan was born in Temanggung, a small village in Java, Indonesia. He graduated from vocational high school and started working for a jewelry company, but soon realized that it was the wrong place for him, so quit his job to follow his dream of becoming a visual artist. He has been coloring professionally since 2011, and has worked on *Doctor Who* and *Sevara*.